Acclaim for this ground-breaking book by Gus Booth...

"Throughout both biblical history and the first three centuries of our own American history, God's minister was often the most significant and influential voice in any community. That is certainly no longer the case today. *Why? What happened?* Pastor Gus Booth takes on these questions and provides a succinct and truthful, but uncomfortable answer. This book is a wakeup call for every Christian leader in America." **-David Barton, Founder & President of WallBuilders**

"Pastor Gus Booth leads the charge in this book, calling for America's pastors to preach biblical truth from their pulpits without fearing government control of censorship. As the first pastor who signed up to participate in Pulpit Freedom Sunday, Gus is uniquely qualified to issue this challenge to America's pastors. Pastors should read this book, and follow Gus' example of proclaiming truth from the pulpit in today's troubled times." **-Erik Stanley, Senior Legal Counsel, Alliance Defending Freedom**

"Pastor Gus has taken the lead in this nation to protect the preaching of the gospel. He is the tip of the spear and the stand he has taken should rally the rest of us to rise up and lovingly fight for freedom of speech right along with him." **-Dr. Jim Garlow, Senior Pastor, Skyline Wesleyan Church**

"The son of a Marine, Gus Booth now demonstrates the courage of a Marine from the pulpit as a pastor. An early adopter of FRC's Watchmen Pastors initiative, it was natural for Pastor Gus to be a part of the first wave of Pulpit Freedom Sunday preachers, which is the subject of his book. God has placed a warrior spirit in Pastor Gus. I pray He has put it in you as well because I believe our pastors are our last best hope in America." **-Tony Perkins, President, Family Research Council**

"In this Fairness Doctrine of another sort, Pastor Gus Booth flips the cry of the dominant culture on its ear with demands for free speech, equality and tolerance for what has become an oppressed minority of its own: The traditional Christian ideology and what once were normative American values. As a gay man, an academic and the former owner of an adult-oriented business who is dismayed that my identity has been hijacked and re-defined by the secular left, I would be a hypocrite of the highest order if I did not stand with him in his fight for the very liberties I have sought for myself." -**Tom Moilanen, M.A. Las Vegas, NV.**

"I have known Gus Booth for several decades. As a former Marine and retired FBI agent, I have witnessed outstanding leadership. Gus' father, Marine Corps Major Steve Booth, distinguished himself both as a leader and warrior and Gus is following in his footsteps. It takes courage to take a stand on an issue which has consequences. Pastor Booth risked both professional and personal standing to battle the overbearing giant that has become our government. It is a classic biblical tale of David versus Goliath. His book is a *"must read"* for anyone who has ever fought the good fight in life and refused to surrender. -**John Ligato, Marine, and Special Agent, FBI, retired.**

SHHHH!

Be Quiet Christian

*How the Church's Message of Love Is
Becoming America's Message to Hate!*

GUS BOOTH

Copyright © 2014 by Gus Booth

Shhhh!
Be Quiet Christian
by Gus Booth

Printed in the United States of America

ISBN 9781629527383

All rights reserved solely by the author. The author guarantees all contents are original and do not infringe upon the legal rights of any other person or work. No part of this book may be reproduced in any form without the permission of the author. The views expressed in this book are not necessarily those of the publisher.

Scripture quotations taken from the New King James Version (NKJV). Copyright © 1979, 1980, 1982 by Thomas Nelson, Inc. Used by permission. All rights reserved.

Scripture quotations taken from the New International Version (NIV). Copyright © 1973, 1978, 1984, 2011 by Biblica, Inc.™. Used by permission. All rights reserved.

Scripture quotations taken from the King James Version (KJV) – *public domain*

Scripture quotations taken from the Amplified Bible (AMP). Copyright © 1954, 1958, 1962, 1964, 1965, 1987 by The Lockman Foundation. Used by permission. All rights reserved.

Scripture quotations taken from the New Living Translation (NLT). Copyright © 1996, 2004, 2007 by Tyndale House Foundation. Used by permission. All rights reserved.

www.xulonpress.com

Dedication

This book dedicated to the Body of Christ in America.
How I love you so and yearn for your action to protect our Lord's gospel.

Table of Contents

Foreword by Tom Moilanen ix
Foreword by Larry Keefauver xi
Preface by Pastor Gus Booth xiii
Acknowledgments xv
Introduction–Heart of a Warrior xvii

Section One: Problem
We Are Losing Our Religious Freedom of Speech!

Chapter 1: Biblically Valued Voters.................................... 29
Chapter 2: Pulpit Initiative – Passionate about Righteousness 42
Chapter 3: Pulpit Initiative – Aiming at Goliath..................... 55
Chapter 4: Fight Right–Preaching the Gospel Brings Freedom......... 70
Conclusion to Part One: The Consequences of Doing Nothing! 82

Section Two: History
How Did We Get Here?

Chapter 5: The Path to Free Speech 89
Chapter 6: Religious Freedom of Speech versus the IRS 101
Conclusion to Part Two: Fight Where the Battle Rages!............. 112

Section Three: Solutions
What Are We Going to do About it?

Chapter 7: Pulpit Initiative – The Responsibility Is Ours............117

Chapter 8: Pulpit Initiative vs Complacency......................125

Final Word..137

Epilogue: Repealing the Johnson Amendment......................141

Pastors Section: A Roadmap for Pastors............................143

Appendix 1 – Keep Your Beliefs to Yourself......................149

Appendix 2 – A Sampling of Christian Writings
               from Our American Founding Fathers................155

Appendix 3 – Two Letters from Pastor Gus Booth to
               Colleagues in Ministry................................163

Appendix 4 – Resources to Embolden You with the Facts..........167

Foreword by Tom Moilanen

A funny thing happened on the way to my father's memorial service. I met Pastor Gus Booth, who serves as the spiritual leader for the Warroad Community Church, a rather quaint throwback to my youth as the native son of another small Minnesota town. Pastor Gus said many a kind word about my dad, I knocked out a couple of appropriate pop songs on a somewhat rickety piano, slipped the kind pastor an envelope and the next day hopped a flight back to my home in Las Vegas, NV, occasionally chastising myself for placing an inappropriately small sum in that envelope.

The power and proliferation of social media reunited us a couple of years later, and it didn't take long to realize I was dealing with not your garden-variety, Northern Minnesota Lutheran minister, but one of those "types" that *my* type is supposed to fear: A non-denominational, born-again, conservative evangelical Christian.

What is "my type," you ask? For starters, I'm gay. I've also held several different positions as an instructor/professor of Communication Studies at the University and Community College levels. If that isn't enough to cast me as a die-hard liberal, I owned an adult-oriented DVD rental store for thirteen years. A gay adult-oriented DVD rental store, at that.

And just to confirm my role as one of the usual suspects, I've spent the last fifteen or so years heavily entrenched in gay media as a columnist, freelancer, interviewer, radio talk show host and, yes, a reviewer of gay adult films.

But, through many e-mails, instant messages and myriad forms of digital communication, it became apparent that the good pastor and I have more in common than many folks of religious or secular persuasion would expect; or approve of, for that matter.

Strange bedfellows, to nip an intentionally suggestive cliché.

This book is undoubtedly the first public acknowledgement of these similarities, as my name appears a couple of times and I'd like to think that a quick proof-read on my part helped yield the repair of a few typos and the addition of some stylistic alterations. And while Pastor Gus and I may not agree in every area, there is a large one in which we do; namely, the freedom of responsible speech and the participation of truly diverse voices in the social and political marketplace.

One of the saddest generalizations made by both religious conservatives and secular liberals is that personal characteristics – such as job, gender, ethnicity, socio-economic status or romantic predisposition – must somehow shape an individual's worldview. But what happens to a society when its members are busier conforming to these prescribed roles than caring for the very soul of their nation?

They wind up attending to the maintenance of their image and neglecting real problems, which is little more than posturing.

A man cannot serve two masters, you know.

Pastor Gus serves *his* master – and his readers – well in this thoroughly reasoned, documented and researched argument for the presence of biblical ethics in the formation of public policy. For those who have a problem with this, may I remind them that all rules and regulations must come from somewhere, and if given the choice of a moral guide, which would they prefer? A book that has profoundly shaped and influenced all of Western Culture for over 2,000 years, or the editorial page of the *New York Times*? I would think that even the most secular, if intellectually honest, would have to go with the former.

And that is precisely what Pastor Gus argues. Congratulations are in order. It's great to see this work come to fruition.

Come to think of it, a funny thing happened on the way home from my father's memorial service, too. I came to know a man that I can privately, publicly and proudly call my friend.

Thank you, Gus, for everything.

- Tom Moilanen, M.A., Las Vegas, NV

A Foreword from the Editor

I rarely write forewords for the books I have the privilege to edit. However, I am convicted and compelled by Gus Booth's riveting exposé on freedom of speech and religion in America to write this foreword. Certainly our founding fathers and mothers were less than perfect in leading America's early formation—but they got fundamental rights into our laws and mindset. So, let's not cast stones at them as some current redactors are doing. Look at the current crop of cultural and religious leaders today. The landscape is littered by their moral failures and political gaffes, corruption, and ungodly behavior. Still, the only way America can right herself is through the power of the proclamation of the Gospel of Jesus Christ. So proclamation can convict and even shame our leaders into doing the right thing.

Truth always trumps lies; light always dispels darkness. Our founders got it right. A society with freedom of speech and religion is essential for this Republic to survive!

Read this book. Get informed. ***Then take action***. Pastor Booth has boldly stepped out of anonymity and into the light. That always invites attacks especially against his views and values. Such attacks will be ignoble attempts to sidetrack the real issues of our essential rights of free speech and the free and public practice of religion. Whether we agree with Pastor Booth's religious or moral views, as Americans we must take action to preserve his and every pastor's or priest's freedom from the pulpit or the street corner to proclaim those views. If we don't, our freedom will be compromised or lost, and so will our boldness to stand up faithfully for Jesus Christ in every cultural venue.

Don't cower in silence. The Johnson Amendment and government agencies like the IRS are wrong! Repeal the amendment. Resist the bullying of the IRS. Be bold. Read, pray, and then act!

Larry Keefauver, D.Min.
Xulon Senior Editor
Bestselling Author and International Speaker

Preface

Fight for Your Right of Free Speech—Or You Will Lose It!

American Christians are taking their right to speak out the truths of the Gospel for granted. Our right to freedom of religion and free speech must be seen through this truth: ***Use it or lose it!***

I am issuing a 21st Century *Declaration of Independence* and *Bill of Rights* manifesto all wrapped up into one soul-searching, heart-penetrating, thought-provoking book. Here's my opening salvo across the Church's bow:

"How pathetic is it for America that our pulpits are better protected by lawyers than preachers."

This book will equip you and your church to protect the preaching of the Gospel and the preservation of biblical morals and ethics in America. As I say later in this book,

"Now is the time as Christians to speak out for free speech to freely proclaim the Gospel and biblical truths about all issues within and outside of Church walls in every segment of culture—politics, government, education, media, finance, business, the arts, religion, and every other venue."

Do you have the boldness, courage, and faith in Jesus Christ to read this book and implement the practical steps provided to save the free preaching of the Gospel in America? If so, buy, read, and act on everything advocated in these pages or you could be hiding in your basement worshipping God in secret very soon!

-Gus Booth

Acknowledgments

The collaboration that has become this book goes beyond its author. I would like to thank first and foremost Dr. Larry Keefauver. Your insights and encouragement made a profound impact in the completion of this book. Without you and your trusty right-hand woman, Pam McLaughlin, this book would still just be an idea.

Tom Moilanen, who too often represents an enemy of Christianity but instead is a friend. Thank you for being the best writer I've ever known.

Mom for the proofreading and Dad for being more proud of me than you should be.

David Barton for being a hero of mine. When my wife told me you called, I almost couldn't believe it. Thanks for calling a no-name preacher to encourage him despite having such a busy schedule.

Thank you to my anonymous donor for living up to your nickname and hearing the voice of God.

Odin Helgerson for being the man who will always have the distinction of being the first purchaser of this book.

Larry Dorman for being the best pastor a person can ever have.

Kim Hruba for tremendous insights from everything from punctuation to marketing.

Veda Constançon whose prayer paved the way.

And last but not least my beautiful Winter Booth, my wife, for driving me to excellence by making sure I didn't put out a lesser quality book because "I just wanted to get it done."

Introduction

Heart of a Warrior

*The **Lord** is a warrior; the **Lord** is his name.* (Exodus 15:3 NIV)

I'm the son of a retired United States Marine Corps Major. Like my father before me, I graduated from the United States Marine Corps Officer Candidate School. My heart is the heart of a warrior that was passed on to me by my father. But not just by my earthly father, also by my heavenly Father.

However, unlike my earthly father, my commission was to lead the fight on the front lines for the Kingdom of God as a pastor instead of as a Marine Corps officer.

Proclaim this among the nations: Prepare for war! Rouse the warriors! Let all the fighting men draw near and attack. (Joel 3:9 NIV)

In 2008, I was honored to be chosen by the Lord and the Alliance Defending Freedom (ADF) to be the first church in the history of the United States of America to challenge the Johnson Amendment. Now I will explore the details of how this amendment prohibits freedom of speech in the church in this book. Let me startle you with the truth from the start: *The greatest threat to America is the gospel!* The gospel declares truth in every sphere of life—religion, business, finance, education, science, media, the arts, and politics. So if the American culture in its supposed "wisdom" declares that marriage is a civil union between two people of the same sex, then the gospel is a threat to that declaration. Do I have your attention yet? So, let me tell you what happened to me and our Church that got our attention.

I simply answered an email from the ADF which led to a series of phone calls and a trip to their headquarters in Scottsdale. I was blown away by how they honored us, the original thirty-three who became involved in what was to become known as the Pulpit Initiative. As I sat there listening to the speakers, I choked back the tears. My mind drifted to a funny, yet sad thought.

How pathetic is it for America that our pulpits are better protected by lawyers than preachers.

Part of my inspiration for the Pulpit Initiative comes from the Apostle Paul whose rights were violated in 65 A.D. We preachers need to stop being wimps and start leading our congregations the way Paul did in Acts 22:22-29.

Paul's rights were being violated, and he was not cool with it. My rights have been violated, and I'm not cool with it either. Paul wasn't even properly accused before he was ordered to be beaten. We, the Church, have been taking a beating for over a generation.

Paul began flexing his muscles against this violation of his rights when he asked, "Is it legal for you to flog a Roman citizen who hasn't even been found guilty?" Paul had been through this before in Acts 16:35-39 when he and Silas were beaten and thrown in jail in Philippi, a Roman colony.

> *When it was daylight, the magistrates sent their officers to the jailer with the order: "Release those men." The jailer told Paul, "The magistrates have ordered that you and Silas be released. Now you can leave. Go in peace." But Paul said to the officers: "They beat us publicly without a trial, even though we are Roman citizens, and threw us into prison. And now do they want to get rid of us quietly? **No!** (**the Holy explanation mark of a Warrior**) Let them come themselves and escort us out." The officers reported this to the magistrates, and when they heard that Paul and Silas were Roman citizens, they*

were alarmed. They came to appease them and escorted them from the prison, requesting them to leave the city. (NIV)

We, like Paul, began flexing our muscles through the Pulpit Initiative (an Initiative to challenge the unconstitutional law that prohibits what pastors can say from their pulpits) in 2008 when I was accused by the IRS of some "supposedly" illegal pulpit activity. They violated our Constitutional rights, and they could have been successful if we had not stood up against the IRS and for free speech in the Church.

Paul's civil government wound up ultimately protecting his rights once they became aware of the violation. Our government needs to protect our First Amendment rights as well. We just need to make them aware of that fact.

In Acts 27:24, God dispatched an angel of encouragement to the preacher Paul that said, "Do not be afraid, Paul. You must stand trial before Caesar" (NIV). I can't help but think that God has dispatched organizations like the ADF to awaken preachers like myself. It's time for us to stand up with the message of the gospel to declare God's truth in every sphere of life without fear. I have decided that no one outside the Word of God or the Spirit of God will ever tell me what I can or cannot say from behind my pulpit. We need preachers who will lead with this kind of resolve and will follow in the footsteps of the Apostle Paul.

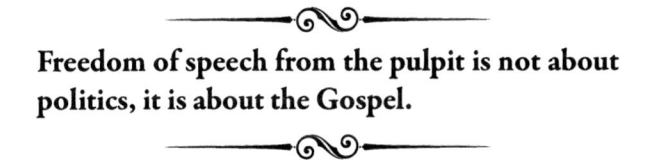

Freedom of speech from the pulpit is not about politics, it is about the Gospel.

If our government can ever tell preachers they cannot say certain political things from behind their pulpits, they can also tell us we cannot say certain theological things.

For example, they could declare that it is hurtful to say that Jesus is the **only** way to heaven. They could declare that is a narrow-minded, discriminating, and hurtful thing to say. We know that Jesus' message is a message of love and not hate. If we want to be able to continue to love people with His message, then we had better stand up for our rights now.

We need to be careful not to fall to the fear of man like some of the preachers did in Jesus' time. Many had heard His message and saw His miracles, but in John 7:13 it says, "There was a lot of grumbling about him [Jesus] among the crowds. Some argued, 'He's a good man,' but others said, 'He's nothing but a fraud who deceives the people.' But no one had the courage to speak favorably about him [Jesus] in public, for they were afraid of getting in trouble with the Jewish leaders" (NLT).

Today, preachers pathetically fear the IRS and other government entities or fear even more so their own congregations saying, "I don't want to become too political and offend the other side of the aisle in my congregation."

My question to pastors is, "Are you their leader or not?"

If you are, then you need to lead them like Jesus, your leader, led you. He was afraid of no man. As a matter of fact He said we are to fear no man, only God.

> *"Dear friends, don't be afraid of those who want to kill your body; they cannot do any more to you after that. But I'll tell you whom to fear. Fear God, who has the power to kill you and then throw you into hell. Yes, he's the one to fear.... I tell you the truth, everyone who acknowledges me publicly here on earth, the Son of Man will also acknowledge in the presence of God's angels. But anyone who denies me here on earth will be denied before God's angels. Anyone who speaks against the Son of Man can be forgiven, but anyone who blasphemes the Holy Spirit will not be forgiven. And when you are brought to trial in the synagogues and before rulers and authorities, don't worry about how to defend yourself or what to say, for the Holy Spirit will teach you at that time what needs to be said."* (Luke 12:4-5, 8-12 NLT)

Believe me, I am not a conspiracy theory advocate or someone who has lost hope in American Exceptionalism. I have simply been awakened to the danger signs throughout our culture which demonstrate the increasing threat to our freedom of speech as Christians.

Introduction

In this book, I will give you an abundance of evidence of how the implementation of the Johnson Amendment that prohibits churches from making any political stands or endorsements is taking freedom of speech away from us. For example, a pastor in Phoenix, Arizona, spent ninety days in jail for having a Bible study in his home. The July 11, 2012 Fox News headline read:

ARIZONA PASTOR ARRESTED, JAILED FOR HOLDING BIBLE STUDY IN HOME; HIS WIFE SAYS IT 'DEFIES LOGIC'[1]

In Hemet, California, two pastors were arrested for reading Bible verses from Romans outside a closed DMV office. The Christian Post headline read:

CALIF. PASTORS ARRESTED FOR PREACHING OUTSIDE DMV, FACE TRESPASSING CHARGES IN COURT[2]

Or what about the abuse of free speech in Orange County, California, when a pastor who is a converted Muslim was arrested for playing Christian music at his table in a public park. The *Free Republic* headline read:

FORMER MUSLIM, NOW CHRISTIAN PASTOR, ARRESTED FOR PLAYING CHISTIAN MUSIC IN CALIFORNIA!?![3]

Our rights are God-given, but if we want to enjoy them and exercise them without penalty here in America as Christians and the Church, we must have the political freedom to declare the truths of the Gospel addressing political wrongs both in the Church and in public.

God clearly tells us we can preach the Gospel, but try to do that in Saudi Arabia, or Cuba, or even some towns in France; you will be penalized

---

[1]. http://foxnewsinsider.com/2012/07/11/arizona-pastor-arrested-jailed-for-holding-bible-study-in-home-his-wife-says-it-defies-logic

[2]. http://www.christianpost.com/news/calif-pastors-arrested-for-preaching-outside-dmv-face-trespassing-charges-in-court-101796/

[3]. http://www.freerepublic.com/focus/news/1567519/posts

for what God has mandated us to do—the same will be true in America unless we maintain the political protection.

Without the Church rising up in our nation and defending free speech, our nation could march down the path of outlawing our freedom of preaching the gospel and declaring God's truths in every sphere of society.

Martin Niemöller (1892-1984) was a prominent Protestant pastor who emerged as an outspoken public foe of Adolf Hitler and spent the last seven years of Nazi rule in concentration camps. Niemöller is perhaps best remembered for the quotation:

First they came for the Socialists, and I did not speak out—Because I was not a Socialist.

Then they came for the Trade Unionists, and I did not speak out—Because I was not a Trade Unionist.

Then they came for the Jews, and I did not speak out—Because I was not a Jew.

Then they came for me—and there was no one left to speak for me.[4]

Now is the time as Christians to speak out for free speech to freely proclaim the Gospel and biblical truths about all issues within and outside of Church walls in every segment of culture—politics, government, education, media, finance, business, the arts, religion, and every other venue. Many of our cultural institutions are coming against Jesus and His message very much like they came against Jesus and His message during the early Church era. So we have this problem, and the solution is protecting the gospel through free speech. In this book, I will give examples of the problems we are facing today. I'll give examples of

---

[4.] http://www.ushmm.org/wlc/en/article.php?ModuleId=10007392

people being sued because they don't want to make a wedding cake for a same sex marriage ceremony. Their religious freedoms are being violated because sexual freedom is winning lately. It is really my belief that one day in this country it will be illegal to say Jesus is the only way. I believe that will happen, and I just don't want to be part of the generation that allows that to happen.

This book will also have the history of how we got here in Section 2. I will explain the whole 1954 decision to make sure preachers cannot preach political messages from the pulpit—which is antithetical to the founding documents and the history of this nation (not to mention the Bible). The third section will outline the solution to keep freedom of speech intact in our nation. It is so important to have freedom of speech. Even though I may ultimately fail, not fighting the fight is not an option for me. I hope it isn't for you either.

The truth is, even as I preach the messages I have used in writing this book from my pulpit, I could be arrested for violating the Johnson Amendment. Our Church could be fined or shut down by the IRS. Like Niemöller, I have thought that this issue wasn't for me or my church, but I was wrong. I must speak out for the freedom of speech for all Christians in our nation. I believe that the gospel is the most important message in the history of mankind, but is not the most important message to the church. Since the gospel has already been accepted by the church, we don't need to hear it again. What the church needs is a teaching on how to protect the sharing of the gospel. Without the church rising up, our nation will continue to move toward inhibiting and restricting the free proclamation of the gospel and biblical truths. Let me give you another brief example.

There is a war between sexual freedom and religious freedom, and those on the side of sexual freedom have found an ally in the IRS. The fight is also between our First Amendment rights and the IRS and other federal, state, and local government entities. For example, in August of 2013, the New Mexico Supreme Court ruled that two Christian photographers who refused to photograph a same-sex marriage had violated the state's Human Rights Act. The Fox News headline screamed:

NM Court Says Christian Photographers Must Compromise Beliefs[5]

This is a good illustration of the bully who says, "Don't step over this line in the sand." Then the bully just keeps moving the line closer to where you are standing even to the point of trespassing on your private property where you have a right to be.

In the same way, our country's government entities have no right to draw a line in the sand and demand you not step over it because some existing ordinance or law has violated your First Amendment rights. I believe churches should step over the arbitrary and unjust lines and call the governmental bullies' bluffs. The Johnson Amendment drew a line in the sand on the church's private realm and forbade churches from crossing it. Since I will be referring to this unjust line in the sand of free speech often, here's a summary:

> *Organizations recognized under Section 501(c)(3) of the U.S. tax code are subject to limits or absolute prohibitions on engaging in political activities and risk loss of status as tax-exempt status if violated. Specifically, they are prohibited from conducting political campaign activities to intervene in elections to public office.*
>
> **IRS explanation of the statute**
>
> *The Internal Revenue Service website elaborates upon this prohibition as follows:*
>
> *Under the Internal Revenue Code, all section 501(c)(3) organizations are absolutely prohibited from directly or indirectly participating in, or intervening in, any political campaign on behalf of (or in opposition to) any candidate for elective public office. Contributions to political campaign funds or public statements of position (verbal or written) made on behalf of the organization in favor of or in opposition to any candidate*

[5.] http://radio.foxnews.com/toddstarnes/top-stories/nm-court-says-christian-photographers-must-compromise-beliefs.html

for public office clearly violate the prohibition against political campaign activity. Violating this prohibition may result in denial or revocation of tax-exempt status and the imposition of certain excise taxes.

Certain activities or expenditures may not be prohibited depending on the facts and circumstances. For example, certain voter education activities (including presenting public forums and publishing voter education guides) conducted in a non-partisan manner do not constitute prohibited political campaign activity. In addition, other activities intended to encourage people to participate in the electoral process, such as voter registration and get-out-the-vote drives, would not be prohibited political campaign activity if conducted in a non-partisan manner.

On the other hand, voter education or registration activities with evidence of bias that (a) would favor one candidate over another; (b) oppose a candidate in some manner; or (c) have the effect of favoring a candidate or group of candidates, will constitute prohibited participation or intervention.

The Internal Revenue Service provides resources to exempt organizations and the public to help them understand the prohibition. As part of its examination program, the IRS also monitors whether organizations are complying with the prohibition.[6]

Notes for the above article.

1. Eyes wide shut: The ambiguous "political activity" prohibition and its effects on 501(c)(3) organizations, Houston Business and Tax Journal, by Amelia Elacqua, 2008, page 119 and 141, referenced February 16, 2012

[6.] http://en.wikipedia.org/wiki/Johnson_Amendment

2. "The Restriction of Political Campaign Intervention by Section 501(c)(3) Tax-Exempt Organizations". Irs.gov. 2012-08-14. Archived from the original on 2 December 2010. Retrieved 2012-09-09.
3. Dorf, Michael C. (6 Oct 2008). "Why the Constitution Neither Protects Nor Forbids Tax Subsidies for Politicking from the Pulpit, And Why Both Liberals and Conservatives May be on the Wrong Side of this Issue". Findlaw.

We just need to take back what is rightfully the right of Christians and the Church for free speech in America. It's time for pastors and churches to fight for the right to declare all biblical truths and the gospel in every sphere of the culture.

> For the pastors and congregations who don't feel called to this fight, we will fight **FOR** you, but we would rather fight **WITH** you.

Section One:

Problem – We Are Losing Our Religious Freedom of Speech!

Chapter 1

Biblically Valued Voters

They set up kings, but not from Me [therefore without My blessing]; they have made princes or removed them [without consulting Me; therefore], I knew and recognized [them] not. With their silver and their gold they made idols for themselves, that they [the silver and the gold] may be destroyed. (Hosea 8:4 AMP)

Pulpit Freedom in America

Meet the Black Robe Regiment, a group of preachers who were fierce opponents of British tyranny and a driving force in the decision of the American colonies to seek independence from England. King George of England had provoked many of these men to leave England because of the unbiblical demands he was making on the church. When they got to America they were powerfully preaching politics from their pulpits. King George called them the Black Robe Regiment because of the black robes they wore when preaching. Most Americans do not know of the role these colonial preachers had in America's fight for independence. Their influence was profound.

It is not an exaggeration to say that if it had not been for the activism of these early American pulpits, our independence would never have been won, and this nation would not even exist. These men were so vigorous in their political involvement that their enemies took notice of them. They did not operate under the misguided philosophy that politics and religion are separate. They saw their role as the mouthpiece of God and that God wants to be Lord of all—every person, every family, every church, every community, every government, and every nation. To say that God does not want His people to infiltrate the political arena is to say that God wants to limit His influence on this nation. Nothing could be further from the truth.

It is my desire to use my pulpit to influence Christians to participate in the election process and allow God to participate as well through you. If God's people don't vote for the most godly candidates, then freedom of speech will continue to be restricted. Too many pastors and their congregations think the way I used to think; they are saying, "Do not take sides politically because if you do, then you may lose your platform to share the gospel with those who disagree politically. After all, the gospel message is more important than the political message." However, using this philosophy is like saying, "Because my family is more important than your family, I will never try to help your family, only mine."

Randy Forbes, Congressman from Virginia, writes about the importance of our religious freedom. Our freedom to proclaim the Gospel isn't a secondary right; it's primary. **Consider the following:**

> *FIRST-PERSON: Religious freedom – A Secondary Right?*
> By J. Randy Forbes Jul 24, 2013 EDITOR'S NOTE: J. Randy Forbes represents the 4th Congressional District of Virginia and is a member of Great Bridge Baptist Church in Chesapeake, Va.
>
> WASHINGTON (BP) — *The First Amendment is a promise that we are free to live holistically, according to the dictates of our conscience. Last month, however, the First Amendment was subjected to assaults seeking to force the fully free exercise of faith into the most private of places: our homes and houses of worship. The intent is simple and fatal: redefine the meaning of religious freedom, making it a secondary right when exercised in the public square or marketplace.*

If religious freedom becomes a secondary right, how will it affect you and your family? What challenges would you face if pressured to choose between your religious convictions and your job, business or livelihood?

The forced compartmentalization of faith fundamentally conflicts with the protection of religious freedom. Our First Amendment freedoms are deemed subordinate, when in fact our Founding Fathers revered religious freedom by giving it the highest form of protection under law. Thomas Jefferson emphasized the value of freedom of conscience when he stated that "no provision in our Constitution ought to be dearer to man than that which protects the rights of conscience against the enterprises of the civil authority."

Freedom of religion is more than freedom of worship. Freedom of religion is the freedom to live every aspect of our lives according to our faith. When individuals are faced with choosing between exercising their faith or defending a lawsuit or paying a fine, they are being deprived of a guaranteed constitutional right. © Copyright 2013 Baptist Press Original copy of this story can be found at http://www.bpnews.net/bpnews.asp?ID=40790

I am convinced that free speech and freedom of religion are essential in our Republic to the preservation of free pulpits to proclaim Gospel truth. Are you?

Should Christians be Involved in Politics?

There is a political battle raging all around us. Martin Luther said: **"If I profess with the loudest voice and clearest exposition every portion of the truth of God except precisely that little point which the world and the devil are at the moment attacking, I am not confessing Christ.... Where the battle rages, there the loyalty of the soldier is proved."**

The point Martin Luther was making is that if you are living in a culture where human sacrifice isn't a problem, then why rail against it? Is the church as passionate about influencing politics as we are about stopping the legalization of abortion? The truth is you can't stop legalized abortion without being politically active. Who we elect into office has a direct effect on whether that disgusting and wicked murderous procedure remains legal in our nation. Therefore, politically charged sermons from the pulpit during an election year are hugely appropriate. Many people call themselves Christians yet they support political candidates that think it is okay to sacrifice a human baby. We need to influence them by arming ourselves with information.

Do we really think God does not want His people involved in politics? Not only does He want His people politically active, He wants them voting for the most biblically accurate candidates. He even wants His people to run as candidates! He also wants us to confront the sin of any candidate or political leader. The Lord sent the prophet Nathan to confront King David concerning his sin with Bathsheba in 2 Samuel 12:1-9. Nathan didn't operate under the principal that religion and politics don't mix. Just like Nathan, the Lord sends us into the political realm.

Jeremiah was another Old Testament prophet sent to confront the wickedness of his culture and the political leaders of his time. Although Jeremiah was a profound patriot, he was in opposition to nearly everything his king did, and as a result was called a traitor, arrested, and threatened. Most of his speeches were made to King Jehoiakim and King Zedekiah.

John the Baptist boldly confronted Herod concerning his sinful affair with his brother's wife in Mark 6:18 and brought public attention to the sinful personal life of that powerful governor. It wasn't just about ungodly political policy, John brought out the governor's ungodly character as well. Jesus also confronted Herod calling him a fox in Luke 13:31-32.

When you make comments about politicians, you are being political therefore Jesus was political. He is our perfect example!

Not so long ago former President Clinton had some of his own problems with adultery. I remember that some people defended him with the argument that his private life had nothing to do with his public life. Yet our Biblical example of John the Baptist preaching against Herod's private life is a glaring example for us to live out today. God needs us to be His voice of disagreement and speak the truth in love.

Nathan, Jeremiah, John the Baptist, and Jesus are four men among others whose examples God recorded in the Bible for us to follow.

When the godly are in authority, the people rejoice. But when the wicked are in power, they groan. (Proverbs 29:2 NLT)

God has given us a country by which we can choose who we want to lead us—the godly or the wicked. If the godly in this country do not work to help the most biblically accurate candidates get elected, then is it any wonder we have legalized abortion in our nation? If our parents, grandparents, and great-grandparents would have elected godly men and women in the early twentieth century, they would not have appointed judges who were ungodly. The appointed Supreme Court judges of 1973 made murdering innocent children legal. Legalized abortion is the result of the philosophy that we shouldn't mix religion and politics. We are now paying for our previous generation's mistakes and roughly fifty-five million babies have paid the price, too.

You know there is another issue that the devil is currently attacking—marriage. Here is information about same-sex marriage in California from the Huffington Post:

> "By a 5-4 vote, the justices held in Hollingsworth v. Perry that the traditional marriage activists who put Proposition 8 on California ballots in 2008 did not have the constitutional authority, or standing, to defend the law in federal courts after the state refused to appeal its loss at trial." From Mike Sacks, Ryan J. Reilly. "Supreme Court Rules on Prop 8, Lets Gay Marriage Resume in California." HuffingtonPost.com. 6/26/2013.[7]

Our political leaders are debating whether or not to legalize same-sex marriage. At this point I need to point out that if all of our political leaders were godly, there would be no debate, but obviously they are not godly. Too many godly people have absolved themselves from the political process. I do not want one of my sons or grandsons to stand at a pulpit someday

---

[7.] http://marriage.about.com/cs/marriagelicenses/p/california.htm

lamenting about what I let happen. The legalization of same sex marriage will erode the institution of marriage.

It's Time to Take Responsibility

Charles Finney, one of the greatest revivalist preachers of American history said, "If there is a decay of conscience, the pulpit is responsible for it. If the public press lacks moral discernment, the pulpit is responsible for it. If the church is degenerate and worldly, the pulpit is responsible for it. If the world loses its interest in Christianity, the pulpit is responsible for it. If satan rules in our halls of legislation, the pulpit is responsible for it. If our politics becomes so corrupt that the very foundations of our government are ready to fall away, the pulpit is responsible for it."[8] Well, I have concluded that my pulpit will not be responsible for it!

Henry Ward Beecher was pastor of the Plymouth Church in Brooklyn from 1847 to 1887 and was an outspoken opponent of slavery from the pulpit. In one of his sermons in March of 1863, Ward stated, "It is sometimes said that ministers must not preach politics. I would like to know how they are going to preach the text from Matthew 20:25-28 without preaching politics. They would have to toe hop, skip, and jump through two-thirds of the Bible if they did not, for there is not another book on the face of God's earth that is so full of commerce and business and government, and the relations between the governing and the governed, as this same Bible. How could it be otherwise, when church and state are one in the whole period of the Old Testament where the revelations were based on the coexistence of these two interests? And yet, in these later days, we have these ineffable men who tell us that we must not preach in the pulpit about public affairs, and who would scourge out of the sanctuary a full half of the Bible. Infidels!"[9]

The Bible is not silent on the moral issues we face in our country today. In fact the Bible specifically addresses these issues. For Christians, God's commands are "non-negotiable." To disobey God's commands is called sin, and voting for candidates that stand in direct opposition to Scripture is

---

[8.] http://www.sermonindex.net/modules/newbb/viewtopic.php?topic_id=47830&forum=35

[9.] http://en.wikipedia.org/wiki/Harry_F._Ward

direct approval of things the Bible commands us not to approve of or participate in as Christians.

John Adams wrote in his diary in 1756: "Suppose a nation in some distant region should take the Bible for their only law Book, and every member should regulate his conduct by its precepts there exhibited! Every member would be obligated in conscience, to temperance, frugality, and industry; to justice, kindness, and charity towards his fellow men; and to piety, love, and reverence toward Almighty God...What a Eutopia, what a Paradise would this region be."[10]

God's Non-Negotiable Commands

> *Now all has been heard; here is the conclusion of the matter: Fear God and keep his commandments, for this is the duty of all mankind.* (Ecclesiastes 12:13 NIV)

The sixth commandment clearly states, "You shall not murder" (Exodus 20:13 NIV). This commandment is about respecting human life. This commandment applies to embryo-destructive research, abortion, suicide, euthanasia, etc. The sanctity of life and the institution of marriage are precious to God. Life in the womb is no different than one out of the womb.

> *And it came to pass, that, when Elisabeth heard the salutation of Mary, the **babe** leaped in her womb; and Elisabeth was filled with the Holy Ghost.* (Luke 1:41 KJV emphasis added)

That word babe or baby is *brephos* in the Greek. This verse is specifically talking about John the Baptist while he was in his mother's womb. In Luke 2:12 the **same Greek word** is used to describe Jesus **after** He was born and placed in a manger. Jesus was out of the womb.

> *And this shall be a sign unto you; Ye shall find the **babe** wrapped in swaddling clothes, lying in a manger.* (Luke 2:12 KJV emphasis added)

---

[10] http://www.constitution.org/primarysources/adamsdiary.html

God makes no distinction in the biblical record between born or pre-born babies so neither should we.

> *There are six things the LORD hates, seven that are detestable to him: haughty eyes, a lying tongue, hands that shed innocent blood.* (Proverbs 6:16-17 NIV)

I don't think it can be said any clearer than that. God hates hands that shed innocent blood, and because godly people lack political involvement it is now possible to legally kill humans that are the most innocent! I need to say to those that say, "I'm against abortion, but I'm not against someone else's right to abortion," I say, "You should be because God is!" I cannot believe we have actually swallowed the lie that someone has the right to murder someone else because they are a nuisance.

Abominable Crime

Are politics important? You bet they are! We need to protect our unborn babies and the first institution that God created—the marriage of one man and one woman. Heterosexuality is the divine pattern for all society. Homosexuality is a deceptive perversion for any society. Historical records show that the founding fathers of our country considered homosexual acts to be an abominable crime. Just weeks after the Declaration of Independence was signed, Thomas Jefferson wrote in a letter that "buggery" (i.e. homosexual) should be punished "by castration." While at Valley Forge in 1778, General George Washington drummed out of his army a soldier who had attempted to commit sodomy with another, declaring his "abhorrence and detestation of such infamous crimes."

Leviticus 18:22 clearly states, "Thou shalt not lie with mankind, as with womankind: it is **abomination**" (KJV emphasis added). Then in Leviticus 20:13 it says, "If a man also lie with mankind, as he lieth with a woman, both of them have committed an **abomination**: they shall surely be put to death; their blood shall be upon them" (KJV emphasis added). Abomination is the strongest biblical word for the denunciation of sin.

1 Timothy 1:10 specifically lists homosexuality as a sin. The New International Version of the Bible translates it as "perverts." The Greek

word used here is *arsenokoites* which means sodomite, abuser or literally homosexual.

We have seen what the Bible says about the sanctity of life and marriage. The Bible is crystal clear when it talks about what God says about abortion—He hates hands that shed innocent blood. The Bible is also clear when it states that homosexuality is an abomination. There is no middle ground for Christians on these issues. We cannot name the name of Christ, claim to follow Christ, call ourselves Christians, and support the things He hates. When you become a Christian, He demands all of your life, not just part of it. He does not exempt you from His commands when you step into a voting booth any more than He exempts you when you step into a grocery store or a gas station. There is no time that we as Christians can somehow set aside God's commands and follow our own way.

If You Really Love Me...

Jesus said unequivocally, "If you [really] love Me, you will keep (obey) My commands. Anyone who does not [really] love Me does not observe *and* obey My teaching" (John 14:15, 24 AMP).

You have read the Lord's commands about the sanctity of life and marriage. You need to study the positions of the candidates. There is no middle ground in any election. If you are a Christian you cannot support a candidate that stands for the opposite of everything the Bible mandates on the issues presented on abortion and homosexuality. Our Lord's commands are not optional. You cannot take them off when you enter a voting booth. Our lives should be marked by the complete and unswerving obedience to our Lord's commands, knowing He commands us out of love. We obey Him out of love.

As you prepare to vote in any election, you must ask yourself: Who is your Lord? Is it the Christ or the culture, the Prince of Peace or your political party? If Jesus Christ is really Lord, then He is Lord over every area of our lives including who we vote for and support politically. It is obvious no political candidate can completely embody the scriptures just as we as Christians will never become perfect while on this earth. However, just as we strive as Christians to conform our lives as closely to Scripture as possible, so we should seek to elect leaders that align their positions with Scripture—especially on the vital issues where Scripture leaves no ambiguity.

As you continue through this book, you will see why I can truthfully and enthusiastically say with Paul, "You know that I have not hesitated to preach anything that would be helpful to you but have taught you publicly and from house to house" (Acts 20:20 NIV).

I just wish there were more men like Paul who are willing to offend for the sake of God's Word. It reminds me of a letter I once wrote to "My Ministry Peers" which I have included in appendix 3. It was returned to me and written across the letter were the words in big black marker: "SHOVE THIS CRAP UP YOUR ASS!"

I didn't mean to offend the pastor who sent it back to me, but inevitably even things done in love sometimes get offensive. Below is a copy of an article concerning this very subject and shows just how out of proportion so called "Offensive Language" can get - even to denying our First Amendment right to religious freedom of speech.

Military Chaplain's Religious Column 'Offends' Atheists
By Lindsey Grudnicki (July 25, 2013)

Lieutenant Colonel Kenneth Reyes came under fire from the Military Religious Freedom Foundation earlier this week for posting a column titled "No Atheists in Foxholes: Chaplains Gave All in World War II" on an Air Force base website.

Serving at the Joint Base Elmendorf-Richardson in Alaska, Reyes was ordered to remove the column from the "Chaplain's Corner" on the site because it allegedly offended atheist servicemen. The MRFF claimed that 42 airmen had complained and sent a letter on their behalf to the base commander about Reyes's crime:

> *In the civilian world, such anti-secular diatribe is protected free speech. Beyond his most obvious failure in upholding regulations through redundant use of the bigoted, religious supremacist phrase, "no atheists in foxholes," he defiles the dignity of service members by telling them that regardless of their personally held philosophical beliefs they must have faith.*

The essay, whose title was drawn from a famous phrase uttered by a priest during a siege in WWII and referred to in a 1954 speech by Eisenhower, was removed from the website after the MRFF contacted Reyes's superiors. Now the Foundation is seeking to have the chaplain punished for his "faith based hate" and for violating military regulations.

No such regulation seems to exist that would merit censoring Reyes, and his column (which, for the record, did not attack non-believers) should be protected by the First Amendment. The MRFF is essentially "saying that the coercive power of government must be used to punish a military office, who is also an ordained Christian minister, for making ordinary religious references consistent with his faith," according to Breitbart.

Townhall has republished the complete text of Reyes's short essay. See for yourself how "offensive" his message is:

> *Everyone expresses some form of faith every day, whether it is religious or secular. Some express faith by believing when they get up in the morning they will arrive at work in one piece, thankful they have been given another opportunity to enjoy the majesty of the day; or express relief the doctor's results were negative.*[11]

Take Action

> *You know that I have not hesitated to preach anything that would be helpful to you but have taught you publicly and from house to house.* (Acts 20:20 NIV).

As I conclude each chapter, I will give you steps you can use to begin to take action in your own church and community. In this chapter I answered some of the questions that as a Christian leader you will need to be able to answer in regard to Christians and Politics. The problem we all are facing is that it is not really about politics.

The real issue is:

We Are losing Our Religious Freedom of Speech!

[11.] http://tinyurl.com/mp4ooxv

Below are the questions you need to be able to answer as you begin to take action in the part of the world God has given you to influence, and the people you are called to lead. You are going to have to take a stand and realize that some of what you do is going to offend some people.

1 – *Does God want His people involved in politics?*

>Think of how you can use the examples of Nathan, Jeremiah, John the Baptist, and Jesus to equip your people for the role God is calling them to have in politics. Be able to explain how Proverbs 29:2 shows God's perspective.

2 – *What if you are brought to trial before the authorities for what you are preaching like Paul was, how will you defend yourself?*

>Read Luke 12:4-5 and 8-12 then explain how you will use these scriptures to help equip your people.

3 – *How do you know what the current issues of the day are that God wants you to* **equip** *your people to deal with and stand against?*

>Read the quote from Martin Luther and explain how Christians are to become loyal soldiers.

4 – *Do you believe that for the Christian, God's commands are non-negotiable?*

>Read John 14:15 and 24.
>Explain how you will use this to equip your people to better obey God's commands thus proving their love for Jesus.

5 – *What are the current issues that are in opposition to God's commands and need to be confronted in your local area?*

>Find scriptures that support the fact that they are in opposition to God's commands. Equip your people to use these scriptures effectively to deal with current issues.

6 – Is your church passionate about influencing politics in the areas of legalization of abortion and same sex marriage? What are you going to do to increase this passion in your people?

Use the resources below to equip yourself and your people to deal with these critical issues.

Additional Resource Material

I will give you a list of resource material at the end of each chapter for additional research.

Here is the list for Chapter 1:

Why You should be Involved – A Biblical Case for Social and Political Involvement by John Eldredge available from the Family Research Council www.frc.org

The Ten Commandments Foundation of American Society by Dr. Kenyn Cureton available from the FRC www.frc.org

Homosexuality Is Not a Civil Right by Peter Sprigg available from the FRC www.frc.org

Local Pastor uses scripture to oppose presidential candidates Clinton and Obama (Warroad Pioneer weekly newspaper May, 2008).

Chapter 2

Pulpit Initiative – Passionate about Righteousness

༄

"I am letting you know that I will not be intimidated into silence when I believe that God wants me to address the great moral issues of the day, including who will be our next national leader." (Pastor Gus Booth, June, 2008 in a letter to Americans United for Separation of Church and State)

Religion and politics are two of my favorite subjects. I have a passion about both of these powerful subjects. However, I have been told I am not supposed to talk about those two subjects because sooner or later my passion will outperform my prudence and somebody is going to be offended or just plain mad. I think though, it is safe to say that Jesus was both passionate and prudent.

Passionate is when there is something or someone that stimulates a strong desire within us. Prudence cautions us in how we conduct ourselves when it comes to our passion.

We are living in a day and age when prudence is esteemed higher than passion. The church has bought into the lie that declares, "You should keep your religion to yourself." Because of this mindset, the church and subsequently God has lost influence in our culture. We are so concerned about offending someone that we are offending God in the process.

Jesus was not crucified because people thought He was a nice guy. He was killed because He was highly offensive. He was not offensive for the sake of being offensive, but for the sake of love. The truth hurts sometimes.

Speaking of hurting, what were the sufferings of Jesus called? "The Passion" was what we call the time beginning right after the Last Supper and concluding with His death on the cross.

We humans are passionate about things. Just go to almost any sporting event and watch the people not the event. Have a World Series party, and instead of watching the game, watch the spectators at the game. Look at their facial expressions.

Being from Minnesota, my family and I are big Vikings fans. Once when my father got mad at a Vikings loss, he threw his Vikings hat in the fireplace in our living room. I was mad too, but also remember thinking, "That was a cool hat; I bet he'll regret that someday." He does. ☺ Passion is a great thing, yet too many are not passionate about what is important in life. For example, when there is an election of any kind, we in this country have the opportunity to choose who will be in leadership. Do you realize that when you vote for someone who gets elected, you can say you gave him or her that job? Yet in too many Christian's lives we have to say, "I allowed that person to get elected by not voting for the more biblically positioned candidate."

A Passion for Righteousness

> *Righteousness exalts a nation, but sin condemns any people.*
> (Proverbs 14:34 NIV)

There are generally two main candidates to choose from in each election. As Christians we need to evaluate those candidates through the teachings of the Bible. We can vote for whomever we want, and that is an awesome privilege we are given in this country. As we determine who we will vote for we need to consider the weightiness and the consequences explained to us in Proverbs 14:34. This means that as Christians we need to vote for the most righteous candidates. So how do we find that out? We take the time to study what each candidate says and does and then compare it to what the Bible tells us we should say and do.

The saddest commentary about any of our recent elections is not that our nation elected unqualified candidates to lead our country; it is that so many Christians seem to be supporting candidates that were openly unrighteous in what they condone and stand for.

For example, we must ask ourselves, how do many political leaders make it into office that believe in and support the sin of murder and the sin of homosexuality? What is the current world view on these two very important issues? What does the Bible say about these two issues?

There have been reports of live-birth abortions when late "in the womb" abortions are not fully effective.[12] Abortion laws often fail to protect against such practices. This is because the people in leadership in our government are opposed to laws that would protect these children. You need to get this straight in your mind because if our government refuses to pass legislation to protect these children, our supposed Christian nation is literally giving a doctor a second chance at killing an innocent, defenseless baby.

How can a candidate call themselves a Christian yet not advance the principles of Christ? Many of our so called "Christian" politicians have defined being a Christian exactly the way the devil would define it. The devil wants all Christians to acknowledge Christ with their mouths yet deny Him with their lifestyles. The Bible repeatedly reveals that what we "do" is just as important as what we believe (Matthew 7:21; Revelation 2:26). Many of our political leaders claim to be Christians with their mouths yet deny Him by their political policies.

Barack Obama openly declared he favors the teaching of homosexuality as a positive lifestyle in our public schools during his presidential election campaign. Yet the Bible says multiple times that homosexuality is a sin. In 1 Corinthians 6:18 is says, "Flee from sexual immorality" (NIV).

"The government is trying to censor me and other religious leaders," Booth told ABC News, "I may be taking on the IRS, but the IRS has taken on the Constitution unchallenged since 1954. I feel like the only law that should dictate what I am allowed to say from my pulpit is God's Law." (June 20, 2008 *Pastor Challenges Law, Endorse Candidates From Pulpit* **by Russell Goldman)**[13]

---

[12] http://www.lifenews.com/2013/04/08/gosnell-worker-baby-screamed-during-live-birth-abortion/

[13] http://abcnews.go.com/Politics/Vote2008/story?id=5198068

In a day and age when our world needs righteous leaders, we cannot turn our backs on God and choose leaders that openly defend legislation that is so obviously against what God's Word tells us is righteous.

When Jesus called the religious leaders of His day hypocrites, do you think He didn't still love them? It was because of love that He publically denounced their lifestyles and their teachings. Jesus even called one of the most powerful leaders of His day what was considered a very derogatory name. He called Herod a fox which meant he was a very conniving person.

In Acts 20:20, the Apostle Paul said, "You know that I have not hesitated to preach anything that would be helpful to you but have taught you publicly and from house to house" (NIV). I believe that it would be most helpful to us as Christians to have the most biblically accurate and righteous candidate in leadership.

Not only do we need to vote for the most righteous candidates, we need to campaign for them. John 4:17 warns us, "If anyone, then, knows the good they ought to do and doesn't do it, it is sin for them" (NIV). God does not want us to remain neutral in this battle for righteousness. That was the deciding thought for me. It was that thought that propelled me to get involved in politics, for the sake of Christ.

> "Booth is free to endorse anyone he wants to as a private citizen," says Rev. Barry W. Lynn, Americans United executive director, "But when he is standing in his tax-exempt pulpit as the top official of a tax-exempt religious organization, he must lay partisanship aside. The IRS needs to look into this apparent violation of federal tax law." (June 11, 2008 familycouncil,blogspot.com/2008)

I used to think, "As a minister of the gospel, I do not want to needlessly offend someone by my politics." I thought that the offense would impede me from being able to share Jesus with them. Then I read the platform for the Democratic Party. That platform is like the "How to" manual for sin.

Read it some time.[14] You will find for yourself many statements that violate biblical truths.[15] Of course, this is not to say there are no unbiblical statements in the Republican Party Platform.

Consequences of Unrighteous, Inexperienced Leadership

There is one more point I want to make about selecting political candidates. Experience! There is a good biblical example of how this works in 2 Chronicles 10:1-14.

> *Rehoboam went to Shechem, for all Israel had gone there to make him king. When Jeroboam son of Nebat heard this (he was in Egypt, where he had fled from King Solomon), he returned from Egypt. So they sent for Jeroboam, and he and all Israel went to Rehoboam and said to him: "Your father put a heavy yoke on us, but now lighten the harsh labor and the heavy yoke he put on us, and we will serve you."*
>
> *Rehoboam answered, "Come back to me in three days." So the people went away. Then King Rehoboam* **consulted the elders** *who had served his father Solomon during his lifetime. "How would you advise me to answer these people?" he asked.*
>
> *They replied, "If you will be kind to these people and please them and give them a favorable answer, they will always be your servants." But* **Rehoboam rejected the advice the elders gave him and consulted the young men who had grown up with him and were serving him.**
>
> *He asked them, "What is your advice? How should we answer these people who say to me, 'Lighten the yoke your father put on us'?" The young men who had grown up with him replied, "The people have said to you, 'Your father put a heavy yoke on us, but make our yoke lighter.' Now tell them, 'My little*

[14.] http://tinyurl.com/mrwmtwu

[15.] http://www.politicalresponsibility.com/platformscomparison.pdf

> *finger is thicker than my father's waist. My father laid on you a heavy yoke; I will make it even heavier. My father scourged you with whips; I will scourge you with scorpions."'*
>
> *Three days later Jeroboam and all the people returned to Rehoboam, as the king had said, "Come back to me in three days." The king answered them harshly.* **Rejecting the advice of the elders, he followed the advice of the young men** *and said, "My father made your yoke heavy; I will make it even heavier. My father scourged you with whips; I will scourge you with scorpions."* (2 Chronicles 10:1-14 NIV)

We have experienced similar leadership under Barack Obama. He has rejected the advice of the Bible and has followed the advice of his youthful and inexperienced counselors. Our country needs the wisdom of an experienced godly leader not a misguided inexperienced leader.

The Bible continues the story of Rehoboam in 2 Chronicles 12:1-4. As you read this, think about the consequences of this unrighteous, inexperienced leadership brought upon these people. Could our nation be looking at a similar situation?

> *After Rehoboam's position as king was established and he had become strong, he and all Israel with him abandoned the law of the LORD. Because they had been unfaithful to the LORD, Shishak king of Egypt attacked Jerusalem in the fifth year of King Rehoboam. With twelve hundred chariots and sixty thousand horsemen and the innumerable troops of Libyans, Sukkites and Cushites that came with him from Egypt, he captured the fortified cities of Judah and came as far as Jerusalem.* (NIV)

Track the progression of kings or leaders from 2 Chronicles 10:1-14, 2 Chronicles 12:1-4, then 2 Chronicles 15:1-2. We have Rehoboam who does evil and King Asa who does right and helps the people turn back to God. King Asa wasn't perfect but he began to move things in the right direction once he realized the truth, and his heart became fully committed to the Lord all his life (2 Chronicles 15:17 NIV).

> Though it's impossible to know all the consequences of creating a genderless society by enacting gay "marriage," we do know one thing for sure: Like clockwork in states that already have gay "marriage" (or even states with only civil unions or other legal arrangements), people who have deeply held beliefs that marriage is only the union of one man and one woman become marginalized and are punished as bigots by state laws.[16]

Actions Speak Louder Than Words

Here is a very important question that we must all ask ourselves as we decide whether or not we should become involved in the politics in our land. How you and I answer this question will determine how we vote, and how our country's leadership votes on unbiblical legislation.

> *Should you help the wicked and love those who hate the LORD? Because of this, the wrath of the Lord is on you.* (2 CHRONICLES 19:2 NIV)

If we do not want to be numbered among those that are spoken of in Titus 1:16, we need to diligently study the Word of God and seek to vote for and campaign for those who are the most biblically righteous. Our actions will most definitely speak much louder than our words.

> *They claim to know God, but by their actions they deny him. They are detestable, disobedient and unfit for doing anything good.* (Titus 1:16 NIV)

[16.] *Keep Your Beliefs to Yourself* by John Helmberger, Published by MINNESOTA Family Council 8.1.2013)

We cannot be afraid of acting. God has not given us a spirit of fear but one of love, power, and a sound mind (2 Timothy 1:7). I want to encourage you to set aside your fear and act in a spirit of love and a zeal or passion for righteousness.

Fear Stifles Passion

> *One who is wise can go up against the city of the mighty and pull down the stronghold in which they trust.* (Proverbs 21:22 NIV)

Fear of retribution can often keep us from doing what we know is right. Fear can stifle our passion for righteousness especially when we think the government has the right to interfere with what we are doing or what we are saying. In Proverbs 21:22 I like to think that we as pastors and Christian leaders are the "wise" ones because we know what God considers righteous and what He condemns as unrighteous. We can go up against the "city of the mighty" which in our case represents the government or more specifically the IRS and the "stronghold in which they trust" which is basically the unconstitutional Johnson Amendment. In the introduction, I reported how the IRS has taken this amendment to attack the non-profit churches on the tax issue. Scripture addresses the tax subject:

> *You are also to know that you have no authority to impose taxes, tribute or duty on any of the priests, Levites, musicians, gatekeepers, temple servants or other workers at this house of God.* (Ezra 7:24)

God protects us when we obey Him even if we are being disobedient to man-made rules and regulations.

> *By the word of the* LORD *a man of God came from Judah to Bethel, as Jeroboam was standing by the altar to make an offering....When King Jeroboam heard what the man of God cried out against the altar at Bethel, he stretched out his hand from the altar and said, "Seize him!" But the hand he stretched out toward the man shriveled up, so that he could*

not pull it back....But the man of God answered the king, "Even if you were to give me half your possessions, I would not go with you, nor would I eat bread or drink water here. For I was commanded by the word of the LORD: *'You must not eat bread or drink water or return by the way you came.'" So he took another road and did not return by the way he had come to Bethel.* (1 Kings 13:1, 4, 8-10)

"I'm a spiritual leader in this community, and spiritual leaders need to make decisions. We need to lead spiritually, and we need to be able to speak about the moral issues of the day and right now the moral issues are also the political issues of the day." (Pastor Gus Booth to Barbara Bradley Hagerty on September 24, 2008)

As a spiritual leader, I must obey God's word even if others are critical or opposed to my actions. We need to obey God's word (protect the gospel) not a man who claims to have God's word (live in peace and don't make waves) or those who erroneously say to obey the government at all costs due to their bad interpretation of Romans 13:1, "Let every soul be subject to the governing authorities. For there is no authority except from God, and the authorities that exist are appointed by God. Therefore whoever resists the authority resists the ordinance of God, and those who resist will bring judgment on themselves." Remember that free speech is a constitutional right. When any government entity abrogates or infringes upon that right, the citizen who is subject to the law of the land should stand up for the Constitution and not cower behind the fear of losing public opinion, support, or even face persecution.

The right to religious liberty should matter to ALL of us. If your deeply held beliefs are being threatened one day, it may be another's deeply held beliefs threatened the next.

As a Christian, speak out for the right of free speech proclaiming the gospel and biblical truths about all issues pertaining to politics, education, media, religion, the arts, government, science, education, finances, and business. Be bold like the early Christians in Acts. You have nothing to fear, nothing to hide, and nothing to lose in Christ if you stand up. If you fearfully act like the German Church did during the Nazi era, you have everything to fear, everything to hide, everything to lose. Be bold and courageous!

Take Action

> *You know that I have not hesitated to preach anything that would be helpful to you but have taught you publicly and from house to house.* (Acts 20:20 NIV).

Are We Passionate about Righteousness?

1 – *How would you answer the question posed in 2 Chronicles 19:2?*

> *Should you help the wicked and love those who hate the LORD? Because of this, the wrath of the Lord is on you.* (2 Chronicles 19:2 NIV)

How you and I answer this question will determine how we vote and how our country's leadership votes on unbiblical legislations. I want to encourage you to set aside your fear and act in a spirit of love and a zeal or passion for righteousness and make your congregation aware of how the people that have been voted into office have been voting on current moral issues.

2 – *Are you one of the wise men spoken of in Proverbs 21:22 that know what God considers righteous and what He condemns as unrighteous?*

One who is wise can go up against the city of the mighty and pull down the stronghold in which they trust. (Proverbs 21:22 NIV)

We need to lead spiritually, so we need to be able to speak passionately about the moral issues of the day. Research the moral issues that are affecting people in your area. Find out what kind of legislation is being discussed in your local, county, and state governments. Let your congregation know what issues on are the table to be voted upon.

3 – *Are you aware of how your local government leaders have voted on moral issues in the past?*

In a day and age when our world needs righteous leaders, we cannot turn our backs on God and choose leaders that openly defend legislation that is so obviously against what God's Word tells us is righteous. You and your congregation need to be aware of how your local legislators vote on key moral issues. Even if they claim to be a Christian, it is important that you find out and let your congregation know where these important leaders stand. Encourage your congregation to write letters to their local leadership expressing their concerns about voting on upcoming legislation.

4 – *Has fear of retribution kept you from doing what you know is right? Has fear stifled your passion for righteousness? Do you honestly think the government has the right to interfere with what you are doing or what you are saying, even from your pulpit?*

We need to lead spiritually, and we need to be able to speak about the moral issues of the day, and right now the moral issues are also the political issues of the day. When any government entity abrogates or infringes upon that right, the citizen who is subject to the law of the land should stand up for the Constitution and not cower behind the fear of losing public opinion, support, or even face persecution.

The right to religious liberty should matter to ALL of us. Does it matter to you? Should it matter to your congregation?

5 – *Are your deeply held beliefs being threatened?*

As a Christian, will you speak out for the right of free speech proclaiming the gospel and biblical truths about all issues pertaining to politics, education, media, religion, the arts, government, science, education, finances, and business? Will you be bold like the early Christians in Acts? Will you encourage your congregation to be bold as well? Check your local newspapers and find out how close this issue of religious freedom of speech is hitting. Share these reports with your congregation. See the resource list after Question 6 to help you find examples of how bad this problem is becoming.

6 – *What do you think will happen if the American Church reacts to the direction the government is taking in restricting your rights to preach the gospel?*

Read about the history of the German Church during the Nazi era. Isn't it time to share with your congregation the consequences of not standing up for your freedom of speech especially in the area of religious freedom?

Additional Resource Material

Appendix One: *Keep Your Beliefs to Yourself* by John Helmberger.

Articles on the German Churches and the Nazi State:

Sharkey, Word for Word/The Case Against the Nazis; How Hitler's Forces Planned To Destroy German Christianity, New York Times, 13 January 2002.

The Nazi Master Plan: The Persecution of the Christian Churches, Rutgers Journal of Law and Religion, Winter 2001, publishing evidence compiled by the O.S.S. for the Nuremberg war-crimes trials of 1945 and 1946.

Matexas, Eric. *Bonhoeffer* Nashville: Thomas Nelson, Inc., 2010.

Chapter 3

The Pulpit Initiative – Aiming at Goliath

Isn't it ironic that pastors get reprimanded as violating the fictional "separation of church and state" myth? Because seriously, wouldn't you think that the IRS is in violation as they try and tell the church (pastors) what to say?

Our nation was founded on and for religious freedom. Our country is now attacking religious freedom by saying, "Preacher, you cannot preach about politics and still keep your tax exemption for your church." I respond by asking, "Now you want me to pay for free speech? That's crazy to me!" On this issue, Jesse Weins writes,

> *It is a contradiction for those who believe in "separation of church and state" to say it's the role of the IRS to scrutinize what pastors talk about in church. A pastor's duty to speak truth from the pulpit is a duty owed to God, not the government's tax man. Churches were tax-exempt long before the IRS even existed. The fact is the IRS shouldn't be allowed to violate the Constitution! (W. Jesse Weins, Litigation Counsel ADF)*

I want to paraphrase for you an account from the book of Acts that will put this issue of free speech and the IRS suppression of it in perspective:

> *When they tied Paul down to lash him, Paul said to the officer standing there, "Is it legal for you to whip a Roman citizen who hasn't even been tried?"*
>
> *When the officer heard this, he went to the commander and asked, "What are you doing? This man is a Roman citizen!"*
>
> *So the commander went over and asked Paul, "Tell me, are you a Roman citizen?" "Yes, I certainly am," Paul replied.*
>
> *"I am, too," the commander muttered, "and it cost me plenty!" Paul answered, "But I am a citizen by birth!"*
>
> *The soldiers who were about to interrogate Paul quickly withdrew when they heard he was a Roman citizen, and the commander was frightened because he had ordered him bound and whipped.* (Acts 22:25-29 NLT)

Here is my modern-day rewording or paraphrase of Acts 22:25-29 in light of the issue of free speech:

> *After the IRS enacted the Johnson Amendment Pastor Gus said to the IRS, "Is it legal for you, Mr. IRS, to say that pastors can't preach about certain biblical issues in a country that has championed freedom of speech?" Gus knew the law and his rights as an American citizen.*
>
> *When the IRS heard this they went to the Commander in Chief and asked, "What are we going to do? Pastor Gus knows his rights have been violated."*
>
> *So the Commander in Chief went over and asked Pastor Gus, "Tell me are you an American citizen?" "Yes, I certainly am," Pastor Gus replied.*
>
> *"I am, too," the CiC muttered, "and it cost me plenty!"*

> *Pastor Gus answered, "But I am a citizen by birth."*
>
> *The IRS who were about to continue to violate Pastor Gus' constitutional rights quickly withdrew when they heard that they (IRS) had enacted a regulation that was in violation of the Constitution.*

For me, this book and the fight I am describing is all about the preaching of the gospel and not about politics. Where it's political is that the Gospel confronts, confounds, denounces any political stance that opposes God's truths. I fight this battle because I don't want to live in a country where the government can one day say, "You can't preach about Jesus. He is too exclusive and offensive. How can Jesus really be the only way to heaven?"

This is not me getting political; this is me trying to protect the freedom to preach the gospel. Fifty years ago everyone agreed that abortion was wrong. Fifteen years ago no one was saying marriage was anything but between a man and a woman. Today if pastors speak about those issues congregations are saying, "Pastor, you are being too political." Don't be one of those congregations. What's next? I fear the day the right of free speech will be denied to Christian preachers and teachers by the government from the pulpits and from any media platform. I fear the day that speaking of Christ and biblical values will be outlawed and even labeled as a "hate crime."

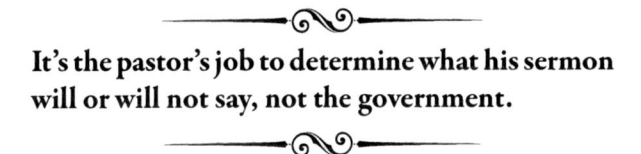

It's the pastor's job to determine what his sermon will or will not say, not the government.

The Johnson Amendment

So why has it become necessary for us to fight this battle? What happened that turned a nation founded on religious freedom into a nation where preachers are being threatened with losing their tax-exempt status for preaching about the moral issues and the immoral leaders trying to gain power in our country today?

"The IRS created a special committee in the 2004 election cycle to specifically enforce 501(c)(3) as a code," Erik Stanley, an attorney with the ADF says. "That committee got bigger in 2006 and bigger in 2008. It's specifically tasked with going after nonprofits and churches on this issue. Couple that with groups like Americans United for the Separation of Church and State, who make this a cornerstone of their mission, and you have a problem. They're on a search-and-destroy mission, to create an atmosphere of intimidation for churches and pastors." (*Aiming at Goliath* by Karla Dial)[17]

It has been said that the income tax exemption is a privilege granted to charitable nonprofits by the federal government because they do good things for society. Karla Dial also states that the government doesn't want charitable nonprofits using the benefit of tax exemption for involvement in partisan politics. They should stick to their charitable missions, the argument goes, and if they want to get involved in political campaigns, then they can just forego the tax exemption. But that makes no sense at all as political action committees are in fact themselves tax exempt. So, what is the real reason the IRS wants to silence the church? Simply because the church has the power to bring freedom and integrity, and presumably the IRS wants control.

Karla Dial gives us some further insights into what happened in 1954 that brought about this radical persecution against religious freedom.

"Since 1954, churches have had their free-speech rights curbed, thanks to the ruthless politics of Lyndon Johnson. Johnson offered an amendment to a Senate tax bill saying nonprofits and churches endorsing or opposing candidates for political office would lose their tax-exempt status. Overnight the free speech pastors had exercised from the pulpit since colonial times was gone forever. Why take on this issue after so many years? Perhaps because Christians are currently looking at their last chance to get the Johnson Amendment overturned, and the forces that would like to see churches silenced forever are gathering steam."

U.S. Senator Lyndon B. Johnson had been openly criticized by two non-profit organizations during his re-election campaign. Apparently the Facts Forum and the Committee for Constitutional Government felt Johnson had been too soft on communism. In the transcript of July 2, 1954, Senator Johnson stood before Congress and said, "This amendment seeks to extend the provisions of Section 501 of the House bill, denying tax-exempt status to not only those people who influence legislation but also to those who

---

[17.] http://tinyurl.com/oh3djca

intervene in any political campaign on behalf of any candidate for any public office" (100 Cong. Rec. 9604 July 2, 1954). There was no further debate, analysis or further committee hearings on this amendment which took away the free speech pastors had been given by this country's founding fathers.

The religious conscience of the nation should be able to speak freely about political issues from the pulpit just as they did before 1954.

"What Johnson did was unconstitutional then, and it's unconstitutional now," says Erik Stanley, an attorney with the Alliance Defending Freedom (ADF), a religious-liberties legal group based in Arizona.[18] "It's time to reestablish churches' right to speak about those issues. The restriction has grown to the point where we really can't ignore it anymore."

Bishop Harry Jackson of Hope Christian Church in Beltsville, Maryland said, "Last summer, our church was involved in a huge campaign against hate-crimes legislation – 'Don't Muzzle our Pulpits.' We felt the bill had the potential to silence the church as we would speak out about biblical morality. I began to see a growing problem-even a greater one than I would have thought in times past. I thought people would rally and say legislation that will limit the church's ability to speak is really bad. Instead, I found a lot of people who were afraid to sign it because their lawyers told them it would bring legal problems. With the way things currently stand, we could find ourselves in a position where people could push some buttons and threaten us in a very unhealthy way. I think it is time for us to get on the offensive."[19]

In an interview on Fox News with Laura Ingraham on August 2, 2008, I told her, "I just feel like the IRS picked a fight with the constitution in 1954 when they put the Johnson Amendment into effect. The constitution has given me a right for freedom of speech, and I just feel like I can say what I want and how I want from behind my pulpit, and I don't have to pay for that right."

---

[18] http://www.adfmedia.org/news/prdetail/4360

[19] http://www.pfaw.org/media-center/publications/harry-jackson-point-man-wedge-strategy#abstinence

Jack Hibbs, pastor of Calvary Chapel Chino Hills in Southern California says, "I've never been one to obey the Johnson Amendment. For me it is one of those situations where I view it as something the Bible speaks about in the Book of Acts. It's much more appropriate for me and my church to obey God than man on this issue. If I serve a God that has to have the help of the government for our calling to be fulfilled, I don't think I'm serving the right God."[20]

"I certainly preach the gospel a whole lot more than I preach any sort of political involvement, but I want to take the gospel into politics. I think politics is corrupt in many areas, and it takes godly men to stand up and say, Listen, enough is enough, and we need to stand up for what Christ stood up for. That is what I am trying to do. I am really trying to represent Christ."[21]

Our Future Is at Stake!

I know that the gospel is the most important message in the world, but the church has already accepted the gospel. Because of the time and season that we are in, protecting the gospel is the most important message for the evangelical body of Christ in America today to proclaim to our culture. This is not an "anti-something" message. It is not that we are against this or that or that we are slamming this or that, but the issue is freedom of speech, religious freedom, and exposing that which completely corrupts in a cancerous way the moral fabric of our culture.

I found that when I was discussing this subject with different producers and reporters, many tend to be very liberal. I realized these guys are huge free-speech advocates as well. They might not like my message, but they believe vehemently in free speech. I told them we are allies on this issue. Though they might not like my theology or my philosophy, free speech is an important issue. I would see during the course of these interviews that instead of being antagonistic they would start to be sympathetic and treat me as an ally rather than an enemy.

Approaching it this way allows us to say that the Constitution, the Declaration of Independence, and the Bill of Rights are being violated by certain laws that are promoting particular issues. The one that most directly

---

[20] http://www.mercurynews.com/california/ci_22251538/preachers-under-fire-politics-from-pulpit-breaks-law

[21] From the Fox News interview of the author with Laura Ingraham on August 2, 2008

affects freedom of speech and religious freedom is the Johnson Amendment. It is like a hole in the dike that doesn't look all that dangerous until that hole threatens to bring the whole dike down. My goal here is to make this book a resource that can educate and motivate people to take positive action.

For example, the gay agenda[22] represents maybe 3 percent of the total population of the USA. Look at how much power they have simply because they have freedom of speech. They have used free speech to leverage the media and public attention. They boldly proclaim that they have the right to say what they want, where they want, and to whomever they want, and I agree with their right to do so.

We are saying non-profit groups, churches, and religious organizations also have the right to express their opinions and their ideas in a free and public setting. In the Bible when the civil government was coming after people who were preaching the gospel, the Christians prayed for boldness (Acts 28:30-31). Throughout the New Testament, boldness is a characteristic of a witness for Christ; we are exhorted to be bold (Acts 4:29, 4:31, 9:28, 13:46, 14:3, 18:26, 19:8, 28:31; Romans 10:20, 15:15; 2 Corinthians 3:12, 10:1, 10:2; Philemon 8, 2 Peter 2:10).

In our day and age when the civil authorities come after the gospel, we as a church pray for protection, not boldness. I am under conviction that the message for us today is to preach the gospel as bold as a lion in every venue about every issue the gospel addresses morally, spiritually, politically, and ethically.

> *The wicked flee though no one pursues, but the righteous are as bold as a lion. When a country is rebellious, it has many rulers, but a ruler with discernment and knowledge maintains order. A ruler who oppresses the poor is like a driving rain that leaves no crops. Those who forsake instruction praise the wicked, but those who heed it resist them. Evildoers do not understand what is right, but those who seek the LORD understand it fully.* (Proverbs 28: 1-5 NIV)

> *When the wicked rise to power, people go into hiding; but when the wicked perish, the righteous thrive.* (Proverbs 28:28 NIV)

---

[22] http://www.huffingtonpost.com/tom-carpenter/the-real-gay-agenda_b_4219250.html

Let's overview some of the areas of free speech we need to address from the pulpit and in our culture with the declaration of biblical values.

The NAMBLA

You may have never heard of the NAMBLA but The North American Man/Boy Love Association is an advocacy group that is working to abolish the "age of consent laws" that criminalizes adult sexual involvement with minors. Yeah? Really? Would you want your child to go to school next to this organization's offices? It is unfathomable in my mind that some men someday won't go to jail if they have sex with a twelve-year-old boy. I bet you that fifty, sixty, seventy years ago some guys just like us said that about abortion. "No way would it be legal for someone to partially birth a baby, shove a pair of scissors into the base of the skull and suck out the baby's brains." Oh, wait that is legal now. When I say that from my pulpit, am I being too political? Remember, pulpit freedom is about being able to continue to preach the gospel; it is not about politics.

ENDA: The Employment Non-Discrimination Act – The End of Religious Freedom in America?

Tony Perkins, President of the Family Research Council asks, "Religious freedom, freedom of speech also referred to as our First Amendment freedoms, how important are they to you as an American? What if they were taken away? Would you miss them? Well, you may not have to wait very long to find out. It's called ENDA – Employment Non-Discrimination Act. I call it the end of religious liberty and free speech in America. According to the First Amendment, Americans are entitled to free speech and the free exercise of their religious beliefs. Yet today more and more Christians are being forced to check their faith and their right to free speech at the door upon entering their place of employment."[23]

"President Obama and his administration have made clear that among their legislative priorities is the passage of the Employment Non-Discrimination Act, ENDA," says, Tony Perkins. "Now let me start by

---

[23.] "ENDA: The End of Religious Freedom in America?" Family Research Council DVD10B01

saying this is not about equality, this is about special rights granted by the government to certain individuals based upon what they do in their bedroom or what they pull out of their closet to wear. Under ENDA, businesses, nonprofits, and even churches, could have to defend themselves against the federal government if they are accused of not hiring or not promoting someone based upon their sexual orientation. As you will see, ENDA comes with a high price tag, but not just economically it is a direct assault on religious freedom. Religious freedom, as envisioned by our founding fathers is more than the ability to worship as you choose within the four walls of a church on Sunday. It was the ability to publicly live out one's faith. What ENDA will do is force a private employer to stuff their moral convictions into a closet when it comes to who they hire."[24]

At the writing of this book, President Obama has taken up a stand for gay marriage. Here's one commentary about this:

"When President Obama came out in favor of gay marriage more than a year ago, he framed it as a matter not of separating church and state but of following Christian teaching: 'When we think about our faith, the thing at root that we think about is not only Christ sacrificing himself on our behalf, but it's also the golden rule,' he said. 'Treat others the way you'd want to be treated.' Senator Rob Portman of Ohio wrote of his switch on the issue, 'Gay couples' desire to marry doesn't amount to a threat but rather a tribute to marriage, and a potential source of renewed strength for the institution.'"[25]

The Senator obviously is defining marriage as a cultural institution and a civil union. The crux of the issue here is whether marriage is defined by the One who created it, the Living God of Abraham, Isaac and Jacob, or if current, changing, and convenient conventional wisdom defines what marriage is. The Senator needs to read Genesis 1-2 carefully and then make clear that he is defining marriage culturally not biblically.

"America today would be unrecognizable to our Founders. Our first freedom is facing a relentless onslaught from well-funded and aggressive groups and individuals who are using the courts, Congress, and the vast

---

[24] "ENDA: The End of Religious Freedom in America?" Family Research Council DVD10B01

[25] "The Quiet Gay-Rights Revolution in America's Churches" by Molly Ball, Aug 14 2013, http://m.theatlantic.com/politics/archive/2013/08/the-quiet-gay-rights-revolution-in-americas-churches/278646/

federal bureaucracy to suppress and limit religious freedom. This radicalized minority is driven by an anti-religious ideology that is turning the First Amendment upside down. America's First Freedom — the freedom of religion — is being pushed out of public life, our schools, and even our churches. The Obama administration no longer even speaks of freedom of religion; now it is only 'freedom of worship.' This radical departure is one that threatens to make true religious liberty vulnerable, conditional, and limited. As some have said, it is a freedom 'only within four walls.' That is, you are free to worship within the four walls of your home, church, or synagogue, but when you enter the public square the message is, 'leave your religion at home.' President Obama and Secretary of State Hillary Clinton have repeatedly echoed this same message in international forums, acknowledging only a right to the 'freedom of worship.' This is no accident, and it has huge ramifications."[26]

ENDA will be the legislation that may probably send me to jail. It is the Employment Non-Discrimination Act which is basically aimed at employers of companies who are led by godly men who would not hire unrighteous people. For example, let's say I run a youth camp and ENDA will not allow me to discriminate against a gay male being a counselor at my youth camp. I have religious freedom and it is my youth camp, so I think I should be able to hire who I want to hire, don't you think? Well, other people would say that is discrimination and because of that you are bigoted. The ENDA makes it illegal for you to have that mentality. I respond by saying, but we discriminate all the time. You who are married have discriminated against members of the opposite sex when you chose one out of so many. There are all kinds and forms of discrimination in our world. Discrimination has become a bad word, but it is not.

We are not a Christian Nation! (anymore)

I believe that the platform which we are to stand on in order to protect the preaching of the gospel is that we are in fact **not** a Christian nation anymore. This country was founded as a Christian nation and the founders were overtly Christian, but not anymore. As evangelical Christians, we try to hold

---

[26] "An Open Letter to the American People" by Kelly Shackelford, Esq. is President & CEO Liberty Institute, Tony Perkins is President Family Research Council

onto our roots as a Christian nation without realizing that we have already lost that battle. I want to try and convince you of that loss. I can talk about the legalization of gay marriage and that it is legal to murder the most innocent people group in our country, the children in the womb. I can tell you how the Ten Commandments are being systematically taken off of all of our government buildings and schools. I can talk about the fact that only 19 percent of Americans wind up in church on any given Sunday. We are supposed to be a Christian nation, and only 19 percent of us go to church! I think all of that is evidence to suggest that we are not a Christian nation.

However, the greatest indicator that we are not a Christian nation is the research the Barna Group did. They have determined through their surveys that only 9 percent of American adults have a biblical world view. Let's just pretend that there is a country out there that has 9 percent believing in the theology of Islam. Would you think that that country is an Islamic nation? Do we honestly think that we could be a Christian nation if only 9 percent of us have a biblical world view? It might be different if there were 35 or even 25 percent.

These are the six basic biblical truths that comprise a biblical world view according to this Barna study:

1 – Absolute moral truth exists.
2 – The Bible is accurate in all the principles it teaches.
3 – Satan is real, he is not symbolic.
4 – We can't earn our way to heaven.
5 – Christ lived a sinless life on earth.
6 – God is the all-knowing, all-powerful creator of the world who still rules the world today.

That is an exceptionally basic biblical world view. My point is there are many more biblical truths that could go on the list about what a biblical world view is, but only 9 percent of Americans believe those six things. I just think, "Gus, you have got to wake up and smell the coffee. You've lost." It was a little tough to admit defeat because I have been on the front lines of this battle for a long time. We also know that in order to be a biblical Christian it is about what you do and not just about what you believe (1 John 2:3; Matthew 7:21).

My point is if only 9 percent believe this, there is a percentage of that 9 percent who don't actually **do** what it is they believe, so the biblical world view of this country probably is even less than 9 percent.

Therefore, because of that fact the greatest threat to America is not terrorism, nuclear weapons, peak oil prices, Islam or any other religion. It is not secularism, humanism, socialism, communism, or materialism. It is not selfishness. It is not the North Korean or Iranian governments or any other government that hates the USA which constitutes the greatest threat. The greatest threat to America isn't even the devil!

The greatest threat to American culture, lifestyle and mindset today is the gospel. Why? Because in America today the gospel, biblical values, and God's law is antithetical and offensive to the average American. The very thing that built this nation is now a threat to it. America is not what it used to be. Today laws are not being written and proposed and even passed that rebuff Islamic Sharia Law, or secular humanism, or socialism. There are no laws being passed to keep those "isms" at bay. In fact, laws are being passed to promote these ideologies.

In our culture today, it is the gospel that is being attacked. Laws are being passed to make sure the gospel doesn't get outside of the four walls of the church. Some people see the Koran as an acceptable viable religious book that we should adopt in this nation; those same people see the Bible as an intolerant, holier-than-thou, antiquated piece of literature. There is a tremendous double standard there now.

I believe Jesus hit the nail on the head when speaking to His culture. His words apply to our culture today as well. John 7:7 "The world cannot hate you, but it hates me because I testify that what it does is evil." So when Jesus walked on earth, His culture was so evil that His message, His life, and His person were hated. The same exact thing is really starting to run rampart in our country today. It has been happening for some years in our nation, but it is really "ramping up." We need to be aware of that fact and address that issue with eyes wide open, not thinking we are a Christian nation. It doesn't matter much how much you say we are a Christian nation, you can't argue with the evidence. It is insurmountable!

Another thing that has been a real problem in this area is that most evangelical churches don't even really know or even care what is happening. The evangelical church has done well at the tail wagging the dog so to speak. There are so many in the church who say things like, "Don't preach anything political. I want theology and a spiritual message, but if you get involved in politics, then you schism the church."

I see there is wisdom in not becoming overly political, but to never say anything political is terrible. There are so many ministers in our evangelical church that subscribe to that mindset. They are just afraid to say something political because people will leave their church. I am not going to be afraid of that. I want to take my direction from the Holy Spirit. I'm going to take input from my leadership team, but ultimately as the leader of my church and an under-shepherd of the Shepherd, it is important for me to not violate the Word of God because I am afraid of somebody leaving the church. Would you want to be led by somebody like that? No, I would not either. Even if I vehemently disagreed on a point, I can respect somebody who says they just don't agree, and this is why I don't agree with you. We can still build the kingdom together as long as what we are disagreeing about is not concerning the deity of Christ or the authority of the Bible.

So I encourage you, the reader, to begin to speak to these issues in church, in the workplace, in political gatherings, on the Internet, and throughout the platforms God has given you to make a difference and be heard. Free speech is your constitutional right and the gospel is your Biblical mandate.

Take Action

We Are Aiming at Goliath (IRS)?

1 – *Do you think politics is corrupt in many areas?*

> If you answered yes, are you willing to stand up and say, "Enough is enough and we need to stand up for what Christ stood up for!"?

2 – *Do you believe the Johnson Amendment has directly affected freedom of speech and religious freedom in this country?*

> If you answered yes, are you willing to boldly proclaim that we have the right to say what we want, where we want, and to whomever we want?

3 – *Do you believe it is time for us as a church to preach the gospel as bold as a lion in every venue about every issue the gospel addresses morally, spiritually, politically, and ethically?*

If you answered yes, are you doing it?

4 – *Now that you have read about the NAMBLA and the ENDA, are you willing to make sure your congregation is informed about these potential threats to our religious freedom?*

If you answered yes, study the information given in the additional resources section and become well informed about the NAMBLA and the effects of the ENDA.

5 – *Are religious freedom and freedom of speech important to you as an American? What if they were taken away? Would you miss them?*

If you believe this is a real issue in our culture today, will you inform your congregation that the gospel is being attacked, and that laws are being passed to make sure the gospel doesn't get outside of the four walls of the church? Will you also research and then inform your people that the Koran is being seen as an acceptable viable religious book that we should adopt in this nation, and the Bible is being seen as an intolerant, holier than thou, antiquated piece of literature? Will you proclaim the potentially destructive effects of this tremendous double standard?

6 – *Is it important for you to not violate the Word of God because you are afraid of somebody leaving the church? Would you want to be led by somebody like that?*

I encourage you to begin to speak to these issues in church, in the workplace, in political gatherings, on the Internet, and throughout the platforms God has given you to make a difference and be heard. Free speech is your constitutional right and the gospel is your biblical mandate.

Additional Resource Material

Aiming at Goliath by Karla Dial

"Thinking more deeply about nonprofits" by W. Jesse Weins- ADF

"Moral and Spiritual Issues in the 2012 Election" by Wayne Grudem, 9-8-12

Open Letter to the American People by Kelly Shackelford, Esq. (President & CEO Liberty Institute and Tony Perkins, President Family Research Council)

Chapter 4

Fight Right–Preaching the Gospel Brings Freedom

Now the Lord is the Spirit, and where the Spirit of the Lord is, there is freedom. (2 Corinthians 3:17 NIV)

In 2008, our congregation became the first church in the history of the United States to challenge what is called the Johnson Amendment. The Johnson Amendment says, "Under the Internal Revenue Code, all section 501(c)(3) organizations (non-profit and churches) are absolutely prohibited from directly or indirectly participating in, or intervening in, any political campaign on behalf of (or in opposition to) any candidate for elective public office. This prohibition applies to all campaigns including campaigns at the federal, state and local level. Violation of this prohibition may result in denial or revocation of tax-exempt status and the imposition of certain excise taxes" (F.S. 2006-17). This IRS law is in direct opposition to our Constitution and our First Amendment rights, not to mention the most important of documents – the Bible. In order to be obedient to the Great Commission, we need to be able to preach. Preach wherever and whenever the Holy Spirit leads! Not when the IRS dictates!

The IRS or any other government entity should not be allowed to limit my freedom of speech or freedom to exercise my religion. But they did. The great irony here is that the IRS wants churches to **pay** for **free** speech by giving up their tax exemption. We are being asked to pay for something that is a guaranteed freedom. Do I as a preacher have to obey the IRS, or can I allow the Constitution to protect my God-given mandate to preach His word?

All of this is an American problem. People in North Korea are not fighting a battle like this. They have such an oppressive government that many Christian families don't even tell their children about Jesus until they are old enough to keep a secret. This is because the government systematically asks kids at school about people like Jesus to see if they are familiar with Him. If the answer is yes, they throw the parents in a work camp somewhere, many times never to be heard of again. They have got serious issues in North Korea because their issues of censorship are so bad. We have a long way to go to get that bad, but does that mean we don't need to squabble about little old tax issues? I will answer my own question with a resounding, *NO*!

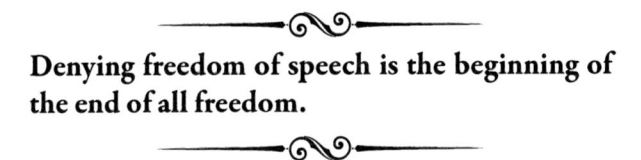

> **Denying freedom of speech is the beginning of the end of all freedom.**

Freedom is the foundational principle that drives the Pulpit Initiative. The gospel brings with it freedom. The gospel is practically synonymous with freedom. So when a government can successfully prohibit churches from saying certain political messages from the pulpit, it is a short trip to prohibit them from saying certain theological messages from the pulpit. For example, they might declare we can't say Jesus is the only way to heaven though He himself made that declaration in John 14:6, "I am the way, the truth and the life. No one comes to the Father except through me." Acts 4:12 declares, "Salvation is found in no one else for there is no other name on earth given to men by which we must be saved." That name is Jesus!

The danger we face if we allow the government to dictate what we can and cannot say from the pulpit could eventually lead to declaring the Bible as narrow-minded and hateful and therefore cannot be used in our Sunday services. It is not hateful. The gospel is a loving message. What would happen if the Bible becomes a hate book and messages from it become hate speech? Pulpit Freedom is all about protecting the preaching of the gospel and not about endorsing candidates. More and more preachers are waking up to that truth.

In the spring of 2008, I was the first one! In the fall of 2008 there were 33. In 2009 there were 84. In 2010 there were 100. In 2011 there were 519, and in 2012 there were 1621 preachers standing up in the Pulpit Initiative. When men and women of God start to realize that the gospel needs to be protected, they rise up. My fear is that there are many "so-called" Christian leaders today who will opt by fear and silence to be part of the generation that lost the freedom to preach the gospel freely. Don't let yourself or your pastor be that, at least without lovingly challenging him or her. Here is what a coming headline may read:

USA Yesterday – Christ Welcome; USA Today – Christ Get Out

Sexual Freedom versus Religious Freedom

A primary issue that the culture is using to try and silence Christians is sexual freedom under the guise of same-sex marriage. It seems weird to me that somehow gay marriage is closely related to religious freedom. I have found though that a law allowing same-sex marriages may require pastors to perform those marriages even when they have religious objections to them. Churches may be required to allow their buildings to be used for same-sex marriage ceremonies, and if the pastors and churches don't allow same-sex marriage, they may be sued for discrimination. Think it can't happen? It already has!

The Ocean Grove Camp Meeting Association is being prosecuted by the New Jersey Civil Rights Commission for discrimination because it declined to open its place of worship for a "civil union" ceremony. While the same sex-couples found suitable beachfront places for their ceremonies, they still sought the legal persecution of the ministry. ADF attorneys are defending the ministry's First Amendment right to use its property in a manner consistent with its Christian beliefs.

"Church buildings are private property and are used primarily for the exercise of religion. As such, the use of church buildings is cloaked with First Amendment protection both under the Free Exercise Clause and the Free Speech Clause. If the government attempts to force a church to use its private property in ways that are inconsistent with its religious beliefs, the government would violate the church's First Amendment rights. Put simply, a church has a right to only allow uses of its facilities that are consistent with its religious beliefs and to deny all other uses. No church should ever feel compelled to open its buildings for use in a same-sex "wedding" ceremony. The best way to protect your church is to adopt a facility usage policy that outlines the religious nature of the church buildings and restricts usage of the facility to uses that are consistent with the church's biblical beliefs. It is always best to adopt a policy governing the use of the facility because a policy is powerful evidence of the church's beliefs and practice regarding use of its buildings. And if your church adopts a policy, it should follow that policy consistently."[27]

Eric Rassbach is an attorney with the Becket Fund for Religious Liberty, a public interest legal group that defends the free expression rights of all faiths. He writes that it is unlikely the government would try to force a pastor to perform a same-sex marriage, but churches that rent out their facilities to the general public could face problems if they refuse to rent to gay couples.[28]

In 2011, Elaine Huguenin, a photographer in Albuquerque, New Mexico, received a request to photograph a same-sex "commitment" ceremony. Because of her deeply-held religious beliefs, Elaine respectfully declined. The two women easily found a photographer for their ceremony, which they were able to have with no problem. But the women decided to attack Elaine for not endorsing their ceremony, filing a complaint with the New Mexico Human Rights Commission, which found her guilty of "sexual orientation discrimination" and ordered her business, Elaine Photography, to pay nearly $7,000 in attorney's fees. ADF has appealed the case in state court on Elaine's behalf.

On August 22, 2013, the New Mexico high court upheld a decision against Elaine Photography after its co-owner, Elaine Huguenin, declined to use her artistic expression to communicate the story of a same-sex ceremony. A concurrence accompanying the opinion concluded that Huguenin and her co-owner, husband Jonathan, "now are compelled by law to compromise the very religious beliefs that inspire their lives," adding "it is the price of citizenship."[29]

---

[27] "Church Buildings and Same-Sex 'Wedding' Ceremonies" ADF July 29th, 2013.

[28] *Churches changing bylaws after gay marriage ruling*, (AP) By TRAVIS LOLLER Aug 25, 2013.

[29] http://www.charismanews.com/us/41712-christian-photographer-who-refused-gay-wedding-gig-pays-price-of-citizenship

Sexual freedom versus religious freedom is coming to a situation near you. If we don't fight on a local, state, and national level the very same thing that happened to The Evangelical Lutheran Church of America could happen anywhere in America. Four years ago, they decided to let homosexual men and women become clergy. Recently they elected their first gay bishop. Most of the leadership of that entire denomination has turned their backs on what the Bible teaches about sexuality.

The leadership in the USA, specifically the Supreme Court, approves of the practice the Lord disapproves of. That is a dangerous thing to do. There are two major cases that were debated in the Supreme Court in May of 2013 with a ruling received striking down biblical marriage. On June 26, 2013, the Defense of Marriage Act (DOMA) was struck down by the Supreme Court in a 5-4 ruling. As National Public Radio reported:

> The Supreme Court issued rulings on two highly-anticipated cases on gay marriage today. By 5-4, *it ruled the federal Defense of Marriage Act, which defines marriage as a union between one man and one woman, is unconstitutional.* In a separate ruling, it declined to take on the broader issue of gay marriage. The court *decided that supporters of Proposition 8, a 2008 ballot measure that had outlawed same-sex marriages in California, did not have standing* to bring the case to the court. NPR's Carrie Johnson explains the Prop. 8 ruling: "By a holding of 5-4 with Chief Justice John Roberts in the majority, the Supreme Court rules the petitioners' lack of standing so the court avoids the underlying issues remands and wipes away the decision by 9th Circuit Court of appeals, which means for now the lower court ruling invalidating California's Prop 8 stands." That means same-sex marriages in California may resume, but the ruling does not have a broader implication across the country.[30]

There are two overriding and major points we need to understand with this battle.

---

[30] http://www.npr.org/blogs/thetwo-way/2013/06/26/195857796/supreme-court-strikes-down-defense-of-marriage-act

Major Point #1 – If the population of America were godly because the church was doing their job, the population would elect godly men and women, who would appoint godly men and women as judges, who would make godly judicial decisions in favor of biblical marriage. That is the representative republic that our genius founding fathers gave us after the study of scripture on how to have a civil government. The Bible was the most referenced book in America's founding fathers' personal writings (See Appendix 2). The church has not been very effective at her job, and that is why we are even debating the definition of marriage. But that can be changed by you and me.

Major Point #2 – There is a battle between sexual freedom and religious freedom. If religious freedom wins, there will still be sexual freedom. It just will not be governmentally recognized and regulated. It is a good thing when the government does not recognize what is sinful. In Isaiah 1:25 God declares, "I will turn my hand against you." The "you" the scripture is speaking of is the whole nation of Israel. So why is God turning His hand against the whole nation? Because of Verse 23: "Your rulers are rebels." To make this point clear, God will judge the whole nation because of the public policy set by a nation's rulers. We will still have gay couples; they just won't receive the benefits of straight couples to which the Bible would say, Amen. If sexual freedom wins, then the by-product of that will be religious freedom losing. Our religious convictions may be criminalized under our discrimination and hate speech laws.

Pulpit Freedom is not about politics. It is about becoming aware of how the culture is attacking the preaching of the gospel by using gay marriage. We need to fight back right where the attack is happening.

Fighting for the First Amendment freedom of religion and speech is more important than overturning Roe vs. Wade.

Fighting for the First Amendment freedom of religion and speech is more important than overturning Roe vs. Wade. Our First Amendment is the bedrock on which we stand to fight to overturn Roe vs. Wade. Without the First Amendment we couldn't even fight for pro-life. With the First Amendment, our founding fathers gave us a wonderful piece of protection. Unfortunately only 1621 (the amount of pastors in 2012 involved in the Pulpit Initiative) of the over 300,000 American pastors have realized that the First Amendment needs protecting. One of my favorite quotes in all of history is, "The only thing necessary for the triumph of evil is for good men to do nothing" (Sir Edmund Burke). Don't be a do-nothing Christian! Please write a letter to the editor this week and encourage all Christians to encourage their pastors to protect the gospel. Pastors and Christian leaders are key to the fight for preserving the right to free speech in this country.

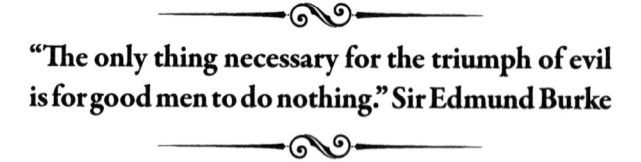

> **"The only thing necessary for the triumph of evil is for good men to do nothing." Sir Edmund Burke**

"It's probably one of the most difficult issues our churches are facing right now," said Doug Anderson, a national coordinator with the evangelical Vineyard Church. "It's almost an impossible situation to reconcile what's going on in our culture, and our whole theology of welcoming and loving people, versus what it says in the Bible."

Simply put, before the Supreme Court had its say about marriage, the Church had its say about how God designed marriage and intended it to function. Now the battle lines are drawn. In the aftermath of the Supreme Court marriage decisions, it is clear that the Church has a lot of work to do.

Jesus said, "Some of you are trying to kill me because there's no room in your hearts for my message" (John 8:37 NLT). Is this where America is going? If the Spirit of the Lord leaves this country, what will happen to our freedom?

> **America was founded by statesmen geniuses but now run by self-serving politicians.**

Fight Right–Preaching the Gospel Brings Freedom

I have adapted some email thoughts I have read.

If you can get arrested for hunting or fishing without a license, but not for being in the country illegally...you might live in a country founded by geniuses but run by popular opinion in the polls.

If you have to get your parents' permission to go on a field trip or take an aspirin at school, but not to get an abortion... you might live in a country founded by geniuses but run by idiots.

If the only school curriculum allowed to explain how we got here is evolution, but the government stops a $15 million construction project to keep a rare spider from evolving to extinction... you might live in a country founded by geniuses but run by idiots.

If you have to show identification to board a plane, cash a check, buy liquor or check out a library book, but not to vote for who runs the government... you might live in a country founded by geniuses but run by idiots.

If the government wants to ban stable, law-abiding citizens from owning gun magazines with more than ten rounds, but gives 20 F-16 fighter jets to the crazy new leaders in Egypt... you might live in a country founded by geniuses but run by idiots.

If an eighty year-old woman can be stripped searched by the TSA, but a woman in a hijab is only subject to having her head and neck searched... you might live in a country founded by geniuses but run by idiots.

If a seven-year-old boy can be thrown out of school for calling his teacher "cute," but hosting a sexual exploration or diversity class in grade school is perfectly acceptable... you might live in a country founded by geniuses but run by idiots.

If your government believes that the best way to eradicate trillions of dollars of debt is to spend trillions more... you might live in a country founded by geniuses but run by idiots.

If children are forcibly removed from parents who discipline them with spankings, while children of addicts are left in filth and drug-infested "homes"... you might live in a country founded by geniuses but run by idiots.

If hard work and success are met with higher taxes and more government intrusion, while not working is rewarded with EBT cards, WIC checks, Medicaid, subsidized housing and free cell phones... you might live in a country founded by geniuses but run by idiots.

If the government's plan for getting people back to work is to incentivize NOT working with 99 weeks of unemployment checks and no requirement to prove they applied but can't find work... you might live in a country founded by geniuses but run by idiots.

If being stripped of our Second Amendment rights makes you more "safe" according to the government... you might live in a country founded by geniuses but run by idiots.

For resources and further encouragement, I urge you to read two ministry letters I have written to my colleagues in ministry which are located at the end of this book. Read them as a letter to you. The freedom of speech you have as a Christian begins with the free proclamation of the gospel from the pulpit within the Church and proceeds into the public arena in every venue of government, education, media, the arts, business, finance, religion, politics, and throughout all platforms of communication in our American culture. Be bold!

Take Action

> *You know that I have not hesitated to preach anything that would be helpful to you but have taught you publicly and from house to house.* (Acts 20:20 NIV).

Are We Fighting Right?

1 – *Do you as a preacher have to obey the IRS, or can you allow the Constitution to protect your God-given mandate to preach His word?*

2 – *Are you concerned that if our government can successfully prohibit churches from saying certain political messages from the pulpit, they might also prohibit churches from saying certain theological messages from the pulpit?*

> If you answered yes, are you going to point out the danger to your congregation by telling them if we allow the government to dictate what we can and cannot say from the pulpit, it could eventually lead to declaring the Bible narrow-minded and hateful and therefore cannot be used in our Sunday services?

3 – *What would happen if the Bible becomes a hate book and messages from it become hate speech?*

4 – *Are you willing to be part of the generation that lost the freedom to preach the gospel freely?*

> If you answered no, what are you going to do about it?

5 – *Are you concerned that a law allowing same-sex marriages may require you to perform those marriages or allow your church building to be used for those ceremonies?*

> Churches may be required to allow their buildings to be used for same-sex marriage ceremonies, and if the pastors and churches don't allow same-sex marriage, they may be sued for discrimination. Think it can't happen? It already has! Sexual freedom versus religious freedom is coming to a situation near you. The best way to protect your church is to adopt a facility usage policy that outlines the religious nature of the church buildings and restricts usage of the facility to uses that are consistent with the church's biblical beliefs. It is always best to adopt a policy governing the use of the facility because a policy is powerful evidence of the

church's beliefs and practice regarding use of its buildings. And if your church adopts a policy, it should follow that policy consistently.

6 – *Has the church been very effective at boldly proclaiming the definition of marriage?*

If you believe there is more we can do, put in place a plan to more effectively deal with this issue starting in your own neighborhoods, your city, and your state. I have provided many resources to help you get started.

7 – *Do you believe God will judge the whole nation because of the public policy set by a nation's rulers?*

If you answered yes, you need to fight back right where the attack is happening.

One of my favorite quotes in all of history is that "all that is necessary for evil to triumph is for good men to do nothing" (Sir Edmund Burke). Don't be a do-nothing Christian! Please write a letter to the editor this week and encourage all Christians to encourage their pastors to protect the gospel. Pastors and Christian leaders are key to the fight for preserving the right to free speech in this country. Simply put, before the Supreme Court had its say about marriage, the Church had its say about how God designed marriage and intended it to function. Now the battle lines are drawn. In the aftermath of the Supreme Court marriage decisions, it is clear that the Church has a lot of work to do.

8 – *If the Spirit of the Lord leaves this country, what will happen to our freedom?*

What are you going to do to help make sure that does not happen?

Additional Resource Material

"Church Buildings and Same-Sex 'Wedding' Ceremonies" ADF July 29th, 2013.

*Churches changing bylaws after gay marriage ruli*ng, (AP) By TRAVIS LOLLER Aug 25, 2013.

Blogs concerning issues of same-sex marriage law suits: http://www.charismanews.com/us/41712-christian-photographer-who-refused-gay-wedding-gig-pays-price-of-citizenship

Information on the Supreme Court Marriage Act: http://www.npr.org/blogs/thetwo-way/2013/06/26/195857796/supreme-court-strikes-down-defense-of-marriage-act

Conclusion to Part One:

The Consequences of Doing Nothing!

The following resources should further convince and convict you. Read them carefully and seriously. Then boldly proclaim the gospel and biblical truths in every venue and all the time!

Frank Wright, Ph.D., President, National Religious Broadcasters concerning the Employment Non-Discrimination Act wrote, "We have to always be fearful of when the government attempts to mandate behavior that will constrain our speech. In the case of ENDA, if passed, it will clearly strain the free-speech and free-exercise rights of religious organizations."

Tony Perkins, President, Family Research Council asks, "Is this your vision for America's future? Pastors fined for simply stating biblical truth in a letter to the editor? Is this the End of Religious Freedom in America? After working here in Washington DC for a number of years, I have seen a very disturbing pattern emerge where homosexual rights become more important than your rights or mine. First, it was hate crime policy, now it's an attempt to secure special rights for employment with ENDA; [next up, was overturning the military's 'Don't ask, Don't tell' policy....] Thomas Jefferson, one of our most well-known founding fathers said, 'When the people fear their government, there is tyranny. But when government fears the people, there is liberty.'" Do you fear what the IRS can do to you? I rest my case. No one wants to tangle with the IRS. That is except those who don't want to explain to their Lord why they did nothing to protect the gospel.

FIRST-PERSON: Religious freedom – A Secondary Right?

By J. Randy Forbes Jul 24, 2013 *EDITOR'S NOTE: J. Randy Forbes represents the 4th Congressional District of Virginia and is a member of Great Bridge Baptist Church in Chesapeake, Va.*

WASHINGTON (BP) If religious freedom becomes a secondary right, how will it affect you and your family? What challenges would you face if pressured to choose between your religious convictions and your job, business or livelihood?

Imagine you run a bakery. You love your customers, have never denied services to anyone and have employed openly gay individuals. One day, a regular customer and her partner order a cake for their wedding ceremony. You are very fond of this customer but believe that marriage was created by God as the union of one man and one woman. Affirming the marriage by baking a cake would violate your belief; you thank your customer for her business and politely explain that you cannot provide a cake. The next week, you receive a letter saying you have been sued under your state's anti-discrimination laws; you face litigation and fines if you continue to refuse to bake the cake. A lawsuit could cripple the business you have spent years to build. What do you do?

What if your daughter's lifelong dream is to be a counselor? She calls crying and says she has been expelled from her program. You are confused. She is an honor student at the top of her class. She received her assignment for a required course, and the client was seeking counseling about homosexual behavior. Her religious convictions prevented her from affirming a homosexual relationship, so to best serve the client, she asked her supervisor to assign the client to another counselor. Her supervisor said she must submit to a remediation program to "see the error of her ways" and change her beliefs or withdraw from the program. What do you say to your daughter?

Maybe your family owns a successful business. You started with one store but now have hundreds of stores across several states. A family of deep faith, your religious beliefs are inseparable from the way you live your lives — including your business decisions. You close your stores on Sundays to honor a day of rest and give your employees time with their families. Though similar stores often pay minimum wage, your full-time employees receive a starting salary almost double the minimum. Full-time employees also are eligible for excellent health insurance plans.

Under the new health care law you will be forced to pay significant fines if your insurance coverage does not include contraceptive and abortive services. Such services, which violate your religious belief that all life is precious, have never been covered under your company insurance plan. You request an exemption but are told your religious beliefs are irrelevant because you are making a profit. You will be fined less money if you offer no insurance, but ceasing coverage would harm your employees. What do you do?

These scenarios are based on real cases happening across the country — a country where people originally came to escape religious persecution. They demonstrate a trend toward a dangerous redefinition of "freedom of religion" to mean simply "freedom of worship."

The forced compartmentalization of faith fundamentally conflicts with the protection of religious freedom. Our First Amendment freedoms are deemed subordinate, when in fact our founding fathers revered religious freedom by giving it the highest form of protection under law. Thomas Jefferson emphasized the value of freedom of conscience when he stated that "no provision in our Constitution ought to be dearer to man than that which protects the rights of conscience against the enterprises of the civil authority."

Freedom of religion is more than freedom of worship. Freedom of religion is the freedom to live every aspect of our lives according to our faith. When individuals are faced with choosing between exercising their faith or defending a lawsuit or paying a fine, they are being deprived of a guaranteed constitutional right.[31]

Randy Forbes gets it; do you? Are you willing to fight, too? If you are a layperson, is your pastor willing to fight for the freedom to preach and proclaim the gospel and biblical truth? I have more motivational and informational material for you to digest. Go to Appendix 4 and get educated, equipped, and empowered. Once you have done that, move into being an active part in how we as Christians begin to deal with this sad moment in American history. Become known as one who fights for our right of free speech.

[31.] *2013 Baptist Press Original copy of this story can be found at* http://www.bpnews.net/bpnews.asp?ID=40790

Section Two:

History – How Did We Get Here?

Chapter 5

The Path to Free Speech

The Ten Commandments and biblical morality were taken very seriously during the settlement and founding of America. "The American experiment," as Dr. Kenyn Cureton calls it, "presupposes the existence of a Supreme Being who instituted a universal moral code which the Declaration of Independence says did not come from kings, rulers, parliaments, legislatures or judges, but from God."[32]

The founding fathers embraced the Ten Commandments in both the legal and all other public arenas; this is very unlike many politicians today who argue that their personal lives should be separate from their public lives. Arguing that way all but makes sure that we have national leaders whom are one way in public and another in private. But wouldn't it make more sense to desire leaders of integrity whom are not moral chameleons? In fact James Wilson, U.S. Supreme Court Justice and signer of the Declaration of Independence and framer of the Constitution, said, "Human law must rest its authority ultimately upon the authority of that law which is Divine...far from being rivals or enemies, religion and law are twin sisters, friends, and mutual assistants."[33]

So the Declaration of Independence declares, "We hold these truths to be self-evident, that all men are created equal, that they are endowed by

---

[32.] http://www.frc.org/booklet/the-ten-commandments-foundation-of-american-society-

[33.] The Works of the Honorable James Wilson, LLD, Philadelphia: Bronson and Chauncey, 1804, 1:106

their Creator with certain unalienable rights." Following up in this context, survey with me what various founding fathers and early American leaders said.

George Washington argued that religion is essential to the formation of morality, "Reason and experience both forbid us to expect that national morality can prevail in exclusion of religious principle. 'Tis substantially true, that virtue or morality is a necessary spring of popular government.'"[34]

Our second president, John Adams said, "It is religion and morality alone which can establish the principles upon which freedom can securely stand."[35] From the same source we read that the Second President's son, President John Quincy Adams commented, "The law given from Sinai was a civil and municipal as well as a moral religious code...most of which have been enacted by every nation which ever professed any code of laws."

President Thomas Jefferson wrote, "Can the liberties of a nation be thought secure if we have removed the only firm basis, a conviction in the minds of the people that their liberties are a gift of God—that they are not to be violated except with His wrath?"[36]

President James Madison, the Father of the Constitution exclaimed, "Before any man can be considered as a member of Civil Society, he must be considered as a subject of the Governor of the Universe." He then prayed that the Supreme Lawgiver of the Universe would guide them into every measure which may be worthy of His blessing.[37]

Rev. Dr. John Witherspoon, President of Princeton and signer of the Declaration of Independence, declared, "The Ten Commandments... are the sum of the moral law."[38] Today our politicians flagrantly violate these commands like Governor Spitzer of New York cavorting with a prostitute,

---

[34] *The Farewell Address: Transcript of the Final Manuscript,* 20 in *The Papers of George Washington* collected by the Univ. of Virginia found at http://gwpapers.virginia.edu/documents/farewell/transcript.html.

[35] *Letters from John Quincy Adams, to His Son, on the Bible and Its Teachings,* Auburn: James M. Alden, 1850, 61

[36] Paul Leicester Ford, *The Writings of Thomas Jefferson,* New York: G.P. Putnam's Sons, the Knickerbocker Press, 1894, 3:267

[37] Isaiah Thomas, 1786, http://www.constitution.org.jm/17850620 remon.html

[38] "Seasoned Advice to Young Persons," February 21, 1762, *The Works of John Witherspoon* 9 vols. Edinburgh: Ogle, 1815, 4:95

or Congressman Weiner of New York taking pictures of his private parts and sending them to friends. That is bad enough, but then Weiner even tried to get reelected, and there really wasn't much of an outcry.

Attacks against Our Nation's Foundation

Recent decades have seen leadership in our nation attempt to remove public expressions of Judeo-Christian religion in general and the Ten Commandments in particular. Nearly all recognition of God or religion, including our core foundation that our rights come from God, have been removed from our schools, courthouses, municipal buildings, town halls, and libraries. This began with Supreme Court rulings in the 1960s that declared prayer and Bible reading in public schools unconstitutional. In 2000, former Chief Justice William Rehnquist said in regard to school prayer, the Court majority "bristles with hostility toward all things religious in public life."[39]

According to Dr. Kenyn Cureton, "The Founding Fathers and Framers of the First Amendment never intended government to be hostile toward religion. The First Amendment was meant to protect the rights of Americans to the free exercise of religion, not to permanently enshrine the government's opposition toward religion or expressions of faith in the public square. If the traditional American idea that liberty comes from God is lost, then from where do our rights originate? From the individual? From acts of Congress? From Supreme Court rulings? If a Supreme Lawgiver has not endowed the human person with inalienable rights, independent of civil government, then those rights can be taken away by government. This is happening today without much of a fight by the Church, except by a few bold leaders. Let's start to become many. So, the undermining of the Ten Commandments is nothing less than an assault on God-given rights, since the only divinely-ordained rights are secure rights."[40]

President John Adams speculated, "Suppose a nation should take the Bible for their law Book, and every member should regulate his conduct by the precepts there exhibited! Every member would be obligated in

---

[39] http://www.law.cornell.edu/supct/html/99-62.ZD.html

[40] *The Ten Commandments, Foundation of American Society,* Washington, DC: Family Research Council BL10D01, 12

conscience to temperance, frugality, and industry; to justice, kindness, and charity towards his fellow men; and to piety, love, and reverence toward Almighty God...What a Eutopia, what a Paradise would this region be!"[41]

Pastors Preaching Politics – Historical Examples

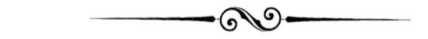

Pastors have a right to speak about biblical truths without fear of punishment. No one should be able to use the government to intimidate pastors into giving up their constitutional rights.[42]

Pastors spoke freely from the pulpit without worrying about tax exemptions until 1954. There are many examples of this all throughout history. In an effort to help us understand what we are in danger of giving up, we will list some of the more influential examples of pastors preaching politics from their pulpits starting with those who helped found this country.

In 1794 sermon excerpts by Jonathan Edwards preached, "We who are employed in the work of ministry, are deeply interested...in the prosperity of the state. It is our business to study and teach Christianity, and thus promote the political good of the state, as well as the spiritual good of the souls of our hearers."[43]

May 29, 1799, Paul Coffin's sermon exhorted incumbent President John Adams, "And the preservation of the life, and eminent usefulness of the President of the Union and the appearance of a [George] Washington once more at the head of our army, are matters of profound gratitude to Jehovah, and of high joy and hope to us... A gentleman said to his friend, with much seriousness, 'Do you believe there is a man on earth readily possessed of all those excellencies which are ascribed to President Washington?' 'I never did till I saw John Adams.'"[44]

---

[41] Diary and Autobiography of John Adams, Cambridge, MA: Belknap Press, 1961, 3:9

[42] ADF 8/4/2008

[43] *The Necessity of the Belief of Christianity* 42-44 Hartford, Hudson & Goodwin, 1794

[44] Boston: Young & Minns, 1799

In 1800, famed theologian William Linn preached sermons opposing the candidacy of Thomas Jefferson for President: "I would not presume to dictate to you who ought to be President, but entreat you to hear with patience, my reasons why he ought not. Consider the effects which the election of any avowing the principles of Mr. Jefferson would have upon our citizens. The effects would be to destroy religion, introduce immorality, and loosen all the bonds of society. I venture it as my serious opinion, that rather than be instrumental in the election of Mr. Jefferson, it would be more acceptable to God and beneficial to the interests of your country, to throw away your vote. Let me further repeat, the single thing intended is to show that he ought not to be honored and entrusted with the Presidency of the Unites States of America. I dread the election of Mr. Jefferson because I believe him to be a confirmed infidel. Sit down now and interrogate your own hearts, whether you can with a pure conscience befriend Mr. Jefferson's election. Whether you can do it in the name of the Lord Jesus. Those who, to keep their conscience clean, oppose Mr. Jefferson."[45]

During the re-election campaign of incumbent President Thomas Jefferson, "Clergymen told their parishioners that a vote for Jefferson was a vote against Christianity and warned that if he won, they would have to hide their Bibles in their wells."[46] Are you beginning to get the gist of this? *During the early decades of our Republic, the clergy were free to preach in their pulpits about the politics of the period.* They freely spoke about political issues and politicians in the churches. So what's with the courts, politicians, and IRS today? Why are they so insistent on limiting free speech about politics and politicians in the churches? I believe they are afraid of the truth; they fear the gospel. They disregard the gospel and biblical truths about morality and ethics because they want to reshape America in their own sinful and immoral image!

"In 1800, as in 1796, Jefferson's religion was a primary target. Yale's Congregationalist clergy-president Timothy Dwight had already set the tone. In a fiery sermon in 1798 he asked why good Americans tolerated such freethinkers as the Jeffersonians? 'Is it,' he thundered, 'that we may

---

[45]. William Linn, *Serious Consideration on the election of a President Addressed to the Citizens of the United States*, 4-35, New York: John Furman, 1800

[46]. Fawn M. Brodie, *Thomas Jefferson, An Intimate History*, 326, W.W. Norton & Co., New York, 1974

assume the same character, and pursue the same conduct? Is it that our churches may become temples of reason...the Bible cast into a bonfire... our children...chanting mockeries against God...?' John Mason, New York preacher, took up the cry. He warned that Jefferson was an infidel 'who writes against the truth of God's word; who makes not even a profession of Christianity; who is without Sabbaths, without the sanctuary, without so much as a decent external respect for the faith and worship of Christians.' New York Minister William Linn lifted quotations from Jefferson's *Notes on Virginia* to shock people and blasted his 'open profession of Deism.'" [47]

Talk about telling it the way it is from the pulpit! "If you did not believe in God, so the clergy argued, you were ipso facto a thief and a seducer.... They accused Jefferson of everything. If the sermons of the clergy were to be believed, there was no crime in the calendar of which Jefferson was not guilty and no unspeakable evil which he had not committed. One clergyman, the Reverend Cotton Mather Smith, accused Jefferson of having obtained his property by fraud and of having robbed widows and orphans. Others warned their congregations that their Bibles would be confiscated if the Republican ogre was elected. They compared him to King Rehoboam, the evil son and successor of King Solomon, from whom the ten tribes revolted."[48]

Using the excuse of the tax-exempt status of churches, IRS is seeking to use the Johnson Amendment to curtail free speech. Such a thought would never have occurred to the political or religious leaders early in our nation's history. For example, during the Presidential election of 1828, "Priests and ministers exercised such an influence over their flocks that efforts were often made to win their favor for one side or the other. A New Hampshire minister delivered in his church an address eulogizing Jackson—an action much criticized by some, but said to have produced a favorable impression on the congregation. Reverend Dr. Ely, a preacher at Norristown, Pennsylvania took occasion to bring in a story to the effect that he once heard Jackson say to a young man of his acquaintance that there was no happiness, here or hereafter, without religion; and the preacher added, he knew that General Jackson had ever lived up to the principles of true religion."[49]

[47.] (Paul E. Boller, *Presidential Campaigns,* 12, New York: Oxford Univ. Press, 1984).

[48.] Saul K. Padover, *Jefferson,* 119, New York: Penguin Books, 1970

[49.] Florence Weston, *The Presidential Election of 1828,* 169-70, Wash. D.C., 1938

During this same election, *The Free Enquirer*, November 3, 1832, reported, "A clergyman in Ohio has lately been preaching politics from his pulpit. In one of his sermons he says that the pestilence which is now raging in our land is a scourge on the people for electing General Jackson as their President."[50]

Not only was the morality of a politician fair game for preaching, so was the issue of war. Polemics accusing a sitting president of treason were issued from church platforms. One case about a fiery preacher was reported, "The preacher was aware that President Polk had said that opposition to the war was treason, and commented: 'Your President tells it is treason to talk so!' Treason is it? If my country is in the wrong, and I know it, and hold my peace, then I am guilty of treason, moral treason."[51]

Today, the government tries to tell us that endorsing a candidate from the pulpit is illegal. That wasn't the case during Lincoln's election. In 1864, a sermon by William A. Stearns endorsed incumbent President Abraham Lincoln, "There is a power in this land hardly second to that of an immense army. It is the wisdom and honesty, and the reputation of it inspiring confidence at home and abroad, which belong to the character of Abraham Lincoln."[52]

Sermons given during the Presidential election of 1884 included, "Cleveland's candor about his youthful relations with Maria Halpin did not help him with some people. Reverend Mr. Ball of Buffalo, claiming to speak for a ministerial investigating committee, went in for extravagant extrapolations after the Halpin story came to light. 'Investigations,' he announced solemnly, 'disclose still more proof of debaucheries too horrible to relate and too vile to be readily believed.' For Ball the election was momentous in 1884, 'The issue is evidently not between the two great parties but between

---

[50.] APS Online 16, NY Vol. 5, Issue 2, ProQuest TCU Library APS Online, Nov 3, 1832; 5, 2

[51.] David B. Chesebrough, ed., *God Ordained This War: Sermons on the Sectional Crisis, 1830-1865* 21 Univ. of South Carolina Press, 1991

[52.] *A Sermon Delivered Before the Executive and Legislative Departments of the Government of Massachusetts at the Annual election,* January 6, 1864, 38-39, Boston: Wright & Potter, 1864

brothel and the family, between decency and indecency, between lust and law.'"[53]

May 28, 1911, *The New York Times* reported, "The Rev. Dr. Joseph Silverman, in a peace sermon in Temple Emmanuel yesterday, praised President Taft for his successful efforts in inducing Russia to admit Jews with American passports. Preceding his reference to President Taft, Dr. Silverman said, 'Teach in season and out of season that the ballot is more useful and effective than the bullet; the plowshare greater than the sword. Based upon the Scriptures, the duty of churches is plain. What grander religion can espouse than that which tries to inculcate by precept and example the lessons of living together peacefully?'"

Sermons opposing presidential candidate Alfred Smith included Dr. Charles L. Fry who asked a large gathering of Lutherans in New York, "Shall we have a man in the White House [Alfred Smith] who acknowledges allegiance to the Autocrat on the Tiber, who hates democracy, public schools, Protestant parsonages, individual rights, and everything that is essential to independence?"[54]

All of these examples are not just the exhaustive research of a few pastors preaching politics from the pulpit. Politics from the pulpit was an every election event by most of American pastors until recently. With prayer and your action, election sermons can become commonplace again. My research in preaching about politics and politicians from America's pulpits has shaped my attitude that we must be as bold as the preachers were early in our nation's history.

Time To Go on the Offensive

In recent church history, Christians have reversed how they handle free speech from the pulpit. Instead of being involved and bold, we have turned away from being bold to being defensive. What I mean by that is when something happens politically that is immoral or unethical from a biblical perspective, we hurry up and try to play defense. When we do this we are just reacting to a demonic strategic plan. I believe that we need to take an

---

[53.] Paul F. Boller, *Presidential Campaigns,* 154, New York: Oxford Univ. Press, 1984

[54.] Christopher M. Finan, *Alfred E. Smith: The happy Warrior,* 209, 219, New York: Hill and Wang, 2002

offensive position now instead of playing defense. We have allowed so much sin in our culture because of our apathy. We have stood apathetic to the threats to free speech. We are almost to the point that instead of protecting free speech we are going to need to fight to try and gain it again. We are not that far along yet, but we are almost there. Like the abortion issue; if in the 1960s we would have protected the wombs of the USA, we would not have made abortion legal in the 1970s. I believe that we must proclaim truth from the pulpit to the culture, and that involves fighting for free speech and protecting the preaching of the gospel even if it means opposing Roe vs. Wade and same-sex marriage. Free speech is a fundamental foundational biblical thing that we need to fight for in this nation.

I also believe that this message of protecting free speech is critical to the preaching of the gospel in America. Of course, the gospel message of salvation is the most important message in the history of mankind. There is no message that even comes close to that. However, in the church we need to do more than just preach salvation. We are preaching salvation to the saved when we need to be preaching the whole message of biblical truths to the saved and the lost. But what we don't have is the mindset to protect free speech in the church like we should. In the evangelical church this message to protect free speech is more important than only preaching salvation—we have the gospel of salvation; we need to preach the whole truth of Christ which sets people and the culture free.

Romans 1:25-27 reads, "They exchanged the truth for a lie" (NIV). I really think that has happened in our national leadership. That is essentially in part what has gone wrong. "They believed the lie and worshipped created things rather than the creator who is forever praised. Amen." There are created things that people worship in our country and other countries all around the world. But in the USA, it is money and self. Those are the biggest created things that people worship. Because they exchanged the truth of God for a lie and started worshipping created things, money and self, "God gave them over to shameful lusts...." That is speaking about sexual freedom. That is what is going on now in America today. This is why a judgment is coming against our nation and upon the culture that has exchanged the truth of God for a lie and allowed created things to be more esteemed than the Creator.

Then in Romans 1:28-32 God indicts the segment of the evangelical church of today that has the opinion, "Well, I would never abort a child, but who am I to say what somebody else would do with their body." It is God indicting the portion of the church that says, "Who cares if gay people want to get married? It doesn't affect my marriage." That theology is an approval of those who practice sin, and God is simply not okay with that. We do not have the luxury of playing Switzerland on these moral issues. When we only play defense, we get scored on. When we have that theology, our enemy is scoring on us over and over again. We simply must engage our culture by lovingly and humbly telling them and living the truth all the while knowing that when we do, we will become hated. But in the midst of the hate, others will believe and there will be some that will be woken up to their apathy.

I'm not painting a very positive future for our nation, but it doesn't mean that God is not still in control and doing amazing things in our culture and in our lives through us and in us. One of the greatest expansions of the church happened under a government that said church was illegal. Read the book of Acts and the crazy expansion that happened during the persecution. It is interesting that when you study church history, the greatest multiplications of any church happened when having church was illegal. What happens in this great multiplication is people get saved and then it becomes more expansive and it becomes acceptable to become a Christian or to be a Christian. The culture accepts it instead of coming against it.

As the acceptance of Christianity gets more and wider spread, outreach gets less and less. Then it is not just acceptance, it is actually an advantage to be a Christian like it was in early American history even up into the 50s in America. There was an advantage to being in the church. If you weren't in the church, you were disadvantaged. It was like being divorced in the 1930s. It almost never happened. There was a negative stigma with non-church going and divorced people. We don't have that stigma anymore.

So this multiplication takes place to the point that we become remiss about the message and stop preaching it. We don't really tell people about it, and so more and more people get hostile towards it. Then we find ourselves about to be persecuted again.

That is where we are at. I got to thinking, "Let's just try to help the persecution happen because the more persecution we get the more the church advances." But that is like saying I am going to sin more so that God's grace may abound and may be prevalent in my life. Paul talks about that in Romans 6:1 asking if we should sin that grace may abound. Of course not!

We could now apply this principle to the gospel; let's allow the gospel to become illegal so that the church grows. Of course not! Proclaim boldly the gospel and biblical truths from within and outside your church walls!

Take Action

> *You know that I have not hesitated to preach anything that would be helpful to you but have taught you publicly and from house to house.* (Acts 20:20 NIV).

How Did We Get Here?

Point 1: Many politicians today argue that their personal lives should be separate from their public lives. We now have national leaders whom are one way in public and another in private. Wouldn't it make more sense to desire leaders of integrity whom are not moral chameleons?

Point 2: James Wilson, U.S. Supreme Court Justice and signer of the Declaration of Independence and framer of the Constitution, said, "Human law must rest its authority ultimately upon the authority of that law which is Divine…far from being rivals or enemies, religion and law are twin sisters, friends, and mutual assistants." Do you agree that recent decades have seen leadership in our nation attempt to remove public expressions of Judeo-Christian religion in general and the Ten Commandments in particular?

Point 3: If the traditional American idea that liberty comes from God is lost, then from where do our rights originate? From the individual? From acts of Congress? From Supreme Court rulings? If a Supreme Lawgiver has not endowed the human person with inalienable rights, independent of civil government, then can't those rights be taken away by government?

Point 4: The undermining of the Ten Commandments is nothing less than an assault on God-given rights, since only divinely-ordained rights are secure rights. Don't pastors have a right to speak about biblical truths without fear of punishment? Do you agree that no one should be able to use the government to intimidate pastors into giving up their constitutional rights?

1 – *So what's with the courts, politicians and IRS today? Why are they so insistent on limiting free speech about politics and politicians in the churches? Are they afraid of the truth? Do they fear the gospel?*

>Explain your answers and how this information is going to help you make a stand for religious freedom and freedom of speech.

2 – *Why should we begin to take an offensive position now instead of playing defense?*

>How are you personally going to do this?

3 – *Is free speech a fundamental foundational biblical thing that we need to fight for in this nation?*

>How are you going to participate in this fight?

Additional Resource Material

Wallbuilders.com has a complete listing of election sermons at http://www.wallbuilders.com/LIBhistoricalwritings.asp

Chapter 6

Religious Freedom of Speech versus the IRS

Jesus replied, "If I glorify myself, my glory means nothing. My Father, whom you claim as your God, is the one who glorifies me. Though you do not know him, I know him. If I said I did not, I would be a liar like you, but I do know him and obey his word. Your father Abraham rejoiced at the thought of seeing my day; he saw it and was glad.... 'Very truly I tell you,' Jesus answered, 'before Abraham was born, I am!" At this, they picked up stones to stone him, but Jesus hid himself, slipping away from the temple grounds." (John 8:54-56, 58-59 NIV)

Can you imagine saying something so offensive that when your audience hears it they try to kill you? Do you know what I find very interesting about this passage of scripture? Jesus knew what their reaction would be and He said it anyway. It is one thing to say something and not know that it will be offensive. It is totally different when you say something you know will offend people. The difference between the two is—Love and Courage!

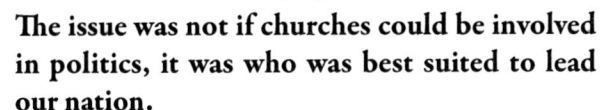

> **The issue was not if churches could be involved in politics, it was who was best suited to lead our nation.**

At this very second God is calling men and women across this nation to rise up and courageously declare our allegiance. The battle lines were drawn in 1954 when a little known senator from the big state of Texas by the name of Lyndon Baines Johnson successfully put into the tax code that charitable organizations could not be involved in the political process. Up until that time churches not only were involved in politics, they endorsed candidates. Congregations expected their church leadership to inform them who to vote for.

The issue was not if churches could be involved in politics, it was who was best suited to lead our nation. The people looked to their church leaders to help them make those decisions. But in 1954 churches had to stop, and a major theology in the Body of Christ started to develop. Churches started to interpret John 18:36 where Jesus said, "My kingdom is not of this world," to mean they were not to get involved in politics. I find it fascinating that there is no single legitimate theologian who would come to the conclusion that this scripture discourages or encourages political involvement. The context of that scripture has nothing to do with political involvement.

Violation of Our Rights

> *When it was daylight, the magistrates sent their officers to the jailer with the order: "Release those men." The jailer told Paul, "The magistrates have ordered that you and Silas be released. Now you can leave. Go in peace." But Paul said to the officers: "They beat us publicly without a trial, even though we are Roman citizens, and threw us into prison. And now do they want to get rid of us quietly? No! Let them come themselves and escort us out."* (Acts 16:35-37 NIV)

If God wanted His followers not to be involved in civil government, He would have rebuked Paul in Acts 16:35-37, but there is no rebuke. Why did Paul and Silas insist that the government officials come and personally escort them from the prison? It was because their rights had been violated!

Our rights have been violated by the IRS, and now I am asking men and women of courage to stand up and fight for the right of freedom of speech. Why is freedom of speech so important? Without it we cannot legally do what God wants us to do (the Great Commission). The only law that should dictate what is said from the pulpits of America is God's law which is clearly explained in the Bible, not IRS law.

So what happened when Paul and Silas engaged their government with their request? Did the Holy Spirit stop them?

We read in Acts 16:38-39, "The officers reported this to the magistrates, and when they heard that Paul and Silas were Roman citizens, they were alarmed. They came to appease them and escorted them from the prison, requesting them to leave the city" (NIV). I have said from my pulpit, "IRS, bring it on!" However, I have also continually told my congregation that the IRS is not the enemy. They are a group of people just trying to do their job. It is that 1954 law that is the enemy.

I have an interesting question for anyone who thinks that churches should keep silent in the area of politics: Why, as a citizen of the United States of America, does my church have to pay for me to have freedom of speech?

I ask that because there are many critics who are saying, "Let the preacher say whatever he wants, but he can't have it both ways. If he wants to preach politics, he can't do it from his pulpit." Their point is that we should exempt ourselves from being tax exempt so that we can preach about politics from the pulpit. Why should churches have to pay for freedom of speech? Churches in the Unites States were tax exempt long before the IRS even existed. It's 'Johnny come lately' to now try to tell pastors what they can and can't say from their pulpits.

It is love that compels a Christian to courageously fight.

When I approached the leadership team of my church about using scripture to oppose certain political candidates and explained that according to the IRS it was illegal to do it, we prayed about it for a week or so and then decided it was the right thing to do. Then I invited the local newspaper to come and write about it. Then I sent the article and a letter of explanation to the IRS and a watchdog organization called the Americans United for the Separation of Church and State. They then reported me to the IRS.

I was then contacted by the Minneapolis Star Tribune (June 12, 2008), Tax Journal Publications, WCCO, WOAY, and other local TV and radio stations. If you Google my name you will find hundreds of stories from around the nation that will pop up, many of which have been unfavorable.

One pastor emailed me and said, "My first obligation is to my congregation not to politics."

I responded, "Well, my first obligation is to Jesus, and I don't think I am doing Him a disservice by talking about politics from my pulpit."

Many people ask me what the response has been from my own congregation because of the infiltration of that erroneous theology that says we should not get involved in politics. I must say I have not received one negative comment from anyone in my congregation.

Biblical courage is a foundational principle of Christianity. Do you think a wimp could have willingly said the things Jesus said? How wimpy do you think it was to die like Jesus did?

However, we must respond to attacks and criticism the way Jesus did, boldly but in love. To fight for the cause of Christ is not more important than to love for the cause of Christ, but you cannot love and not fight. It is love that compels a Christian to courageously fight.

Live a life in which God can say about you, as He did about the political leader, King David, "He will do everything I want him to do" (Acts 13:22). All men die, but few men truly live for what they believe!

A Christian View of Government

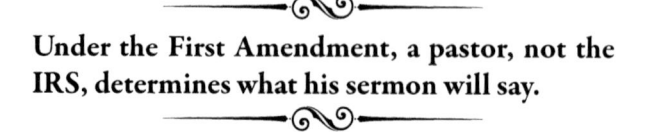

Under the First Amendment, a pastor, not the IRS, determines what his sermon will say.

So what exactly does the First Amendment say? The First Amendment of the Constitution provides that "Congress shall make no law respecting an establishment of religion or prohibiting the free exercise thereof." The first clause is referred to as the Establishment Clause and the second is the Free Exercise Clause. The Establishment Clause prohibits government sponsorship of religion. Central to this prohibition are the concepts of government neutrality and the separation of a state-run church. The Supreme Court has held that the Free Exercise Clause of the First Amendment is an absolute prohibition against the regulation of religious beliefs. The First Amendment provides substantial protection for lawful conduct grounded on religious beliefs. However, the government may limit religiously motivated conduct when the limitation is essential to accomplish an overriding governmental interest (taken from *Statement of Administrative and Constitutional Rights*).

"Politics is defined as 'the art or science of government.' Given the respect the Bible accords to government, why has the church shied away from politics? There are many reasons, but foremost among them is the confusion surrounding the New Testament teaching on civil government," says Professor John Eldredge.

British theologian C.E.B. Cranfield says, "The Herodians, trying to trap Jesus, asked Him if it is right to pay taxes to the Roman government. Jesus responded, 'Render unto Caesar what is Caesar's, and to God what is God's.' (Mark 12:13-17) The word 'render' carries a sense of duty or obligation. Christ commands His hearers to do their duty to civil government, and in the United States, that means participation in the political process."[55]

Charles Finney, the great nineteenth century evangelist, taught his followers that Christians have a moral duty to oppose government when government fails to do the will of God.[56]

Section 7611 of the Internal Revenue Code provides specific protection for organizations claiming to be churches or conventions or associations of churches.[57] However, groups like Americans United for the Separation of Church and State intentionally trigger IRS investigations in an attempt to silence churches through fear, intimidation, and disinformation. I feel it's a direct contradiction for such groups to say that they believe in the separation of church and state, and then say it is the role of the IRS to decide what pastors can or cannot talk about from their pulpits.

The IRS shouldn't be allowed to violate the Constitution by demanding that a church give up its tax-exempt status because their pastor exercises his First Amendment rights of free speech and free religion from his pulpit. IRS rules don't trump the Constitution and the First Amendment certainly trumps the Johnson Amendment.

[55.] C.E.B. Cranfield, "The Christian's Political Responsibility According to the New Testament," *Scottish Journal of Theology* 15, 1962, pp.176-192.

[56.] Francis Schaeffer, *A Christian Manifesto*, Westchester, IL: Crossway, 1981, p.87.

[57.] http://www.irs.gov/irm/part4/irm_04-076-007.html

This is about a pastor's right to religious free speech. It is not about politicking. A pastor should not be forced to step out of his pulpit to speak biblical truths about candidates and their positions. Every pastor has a moral obligation to speak biblical truth from his pulpit. Congregations have the right to hear uncensored biblical truth about all aspects of life including political candidates and their platforms. Politicians shouldn't think that they get a free pass from moral scrutiny.

Attacks against Churches and Ministries

"Religious hostility against churches and ministries represents a new front that secularism has opened against religious liberty. Only five years ago, the idea that the federal government would argue before the Supreme Court that it could regulate churches to the extent of determining who a church may choose as its pastor was unthinkable, yet the government made that very argument—effectively arguing that the religious liberty clauses of the First Amendment are meaningless" (*Hosanna-Tabor Evangelical Lutheran Church & School v. EEOC*). Not only did the government, for the first time, argue that it may regulate churches and determine qualifications for pastors, but the past ten years have seen an explosion in cases involving local governments discriminating against churches, particularly in the local governments' use of zoning laws and granting of permits.

The following cases illustrate this new front in the secularists' war on religious liberty:

Hosanna-Tabor Evangelical Lutheran Church & School v. EEOC: A private Christian school fired Cheryl Perich, a minister and a teacher at Hosanna-Tabor Lutheran School, for threatening to sue the school after she was asked not to return because she had narcolepsy. Perich sued under the Americans with Disabilities Act. In response, the school argued its right to hire or fire Perich based on the "ministerial exception," which legally protects the rights of churches to select its religious leaders without government interference. The Justice Department argued that the "ministerial exception" does not exist and the government may regulate churches' selection of pastors. The U.S. Supreme Court unanimously upheld the ministerial exception and specified that government regulation of the hiring and firing of ministry leaders would violate both the Free Exercise Clause and the Establishment Clause.

HEB Ministries, Inc. v. Texas Higher Education Coordinating Bd.: A state passed a law forcing all seminaries to get state approval of their curriculum, board members, and professors. The state fined Tyndale Seminary $173,000 for using the word "seminary" and issuing theological degrees without government approval. The ministry filed a suit to prohibit the government's attempts to control religious training. Both the district court and the court of appeals upheld the law. Finally, after nine years of suffering and losses, the state Supreme Court reversed and held that the law violated the First Amendment and state Constitution.

While this shows that religious hostility in the United States is dramatically increasing, it also shows that those persons and organizations, like the Liberty Institute and the Family Research Council that stand up for religious liberty are winning. When those who value religious liberty fight, they push back the secularists' agenda. While *Hosanna-Tabor* is a stunning example of the executive branch's rejection of religious liberty, the Supreme Court unanimously held that churches are free from government control. Furthermore, for the first time in *Hosanna-Tabor,* the Supreme Court held that *both* the Free Exercise Clause and the Establishment Clause provide protection for religious liberty, greatly strengthening the Establishment Clause as a tool to protect our freedom. The secularist agenda only advances when those who love liberty are apathetic. Let this be a call to stand for religious liberty in these United States."[58]

The following brief article by Nathan Oppman really brings into sharp focus the issue at this point.

Why Is God Such a Big Deal? *by Nathan Oppman Sept. 21, 2012 Family Research Council*

[58.] www.religioushostility.org; Liberty Institute, 2001 West Plano Parkway, Suite 1600, Plano, TX 75075

There has been much talk regarding the use of God in the major party platforms. One simple word contributed to a major firestorm at the Democratic convention. In a recent column, Stephen Prothero, a Boston University religion scholar, said he wished for a more humble expression of faith and less use of God as a prop. He calls our Constitution godless, in support of his argument that God should not be in the party platforms.

So is he right? Well perhaps partly in that we should not use God as a prop for anything but as the foundation for everything. To call our Constitution godless simply because God is not mentioned would be like calling the Book of Esther in the Scriptures godless because God is not mentioned. Principles come from somewhere. From whom did the Founders think we receive the blessings of liberty? If being godly meant simply referring to God, then we are indeed a very godly nation. But I think we all know it goes a lot deeper.

No matter how hard one tries to remain secular, God seems to come up in American culture. From health care to football (courtesy of Tim Tebow) God pops up in discussion. It is not merely using God as a prop but recognizing that He is the foundation of all order in the Universe. If our rights and potential come from God then we have immense value. If they come from government, they can be ignored and destroyed. If they come from God, they should be recognized and protected. God must be recognized, or all we have held dear for so long in America is potentially up for debate. If the Declaration was incorrect in saying the inalienable rights of life, liberty, and the pursuit of happiness are self-evident rights from God endowed on every man, then much is at stake.

If God is taken out of the equation, then one could make a utilitarian argument for killing those who were disabled or simply unproductive. Instead of debating how to help the poor and infirm, we could be debating how to dispose of them because of cost and inconvenience. One could limit the pursuit of happiness by restricting religious liberty and dictating to people what they should believe and how to apply that belief.

The gospel message isn't just about Jesus Christ saving us from our sins and giving us eternal life. It's about all of life. The Sermon on the Mount is filled with ethical and moral teaching. The New Testament writings are filled with ethical and moral instructions rooted in the Old Testament Law. In Luke 4, Jesus declared that He had come to set the captives free. Who are the captives? Anyone who is in sin and iniquity as a result of transgressing God's laws is a captive. Jesus did not come to do away with the law but to fulfill it. That means, that a life in Christ embodies the whole moral and ethical code of holiness established when God declares, "Be holy as I am holy" (1 Peter 1:16; Leviticus 11:44).

It's true that our culture has moved away from absolute truth revealed by God in the Scriptures to moral relativism which compromises Christian morality in every situation. Absolute truth revealed by God is true for all people, at all times, and in all situations. Relativism says truth is what's true for some people, at some times, in some situations. The freedom to preach absolute truth from our pulpits is essential for the gospel to be proclaimed in America.

Lest you doubt that God plays the critical role in contemporary political issues, I offer some thoughts. In the debate over abortion, those who don't answer the fundamental question of when life begins are left to talk about the cost to the mother of raising an unwanted baby, of a woman's choice, or of privacy. Of course, these all become secondary concerns if God grants a baby a right to life from conception, and it is an inalienable right. In godless regimes such as North Korea and China, you have the untold slaughter of many through forced abortions, prison camp killings, and general government purges. All of this is in the name of some greater good (utilitarianism or despotism) espoused by the ruler or ruling party.

In this country, people like Margaret Sanger, founder of Planned Parenthood, argued that some should be forcibly sterilized if they had bad blood lines. If God doesn't grant liberty, then people are bound to be ruled by the government and the changing views its members espouse. The recent health care law passed by Congress and the President told many organizations who believe that abortion and contraception are wrong that they had to believe something else because the government said so. Cases have come up repeatedly about whether prayers and religious symbols should be allowed in the public square. Even the definition of marriage can be changed by a few members of a court.

Why is government so important when it comes to the rights of man? Because of a less quoted phrase in the Declaration after the statements on inalienable rights, "that to secure these rights."

The government exists to protect us from those who would infringe on our God-given rights and to promote a culture that praises good things.

I'm thankful we still care about having God in our party platforms, but even more importantly may He be at the heart of our great Republic and the policies we promote. The moment a government forgets the God of the Bible is the moment it becomes god. And that is a scary thought. As American citizens, Christians must develop a mindset that adopts the precept that the God of the Bible is the author of absolute truth for all of life including government, finance, business, the arts, religion, culture, education, media, and politics.

"Every system of thought begins with some ultimate principle. If it does not begin with God, it will begin with some dimension of creation—the material, the spiritual, the biological, the empirical, or whatever. Some aspect of created reality will be "absolutized" or put forth as the ground and source of everything else—the uncaused cause, the self-existent. To use religious language, this ultimate principle functions as the divine, if we define that term to mean the one thing upon which all else depends for existence. This starting assumption has to be accepted by faith, not by prior reasoning. (Otherwise it is not really the ultimate starting point for all reasoning—something else is, and we have to dig deeper and start there instead.) In this sense, we could say that every alternative to Christianity is a religion."[59]

What Nancy Pearcey is saying here leads to the conclusion that every philosophy outside of Christianity, including political mindsets that do not embrace biblical truths, are competing religions. Of course, alternative mindsets in our culture want to shut down the free-speech right of Christians to declare the absolute truth of the gospel.

---

[59] Pearcey, Nancy; Phillip E. Johnson (2008-03-31). Total Truth: Liberating Christianity from Its Cultural Captivity (Kindle Locations 964-969). Good News Publishers/ Crossway Books. Kindle Edition.

Conclusion to Part Two

Fight Where the Battle Rages!

The church needs to stay focused on what's really important. Protecting the gospel! Back in 1917, as the Bolsheviks grabbed the reins of power through a revolution in Russia, the priests in the Orthodox Church were in a heated debate over how long the tassels should be on their robes. They ignored the Bolshevik revolution, and instead, split their church arguing over this trivial matter!

We can all rally around protecting the gospel. We need to fight where the battle rages! How do we do that? In the next section, I will address the strategies and solutions we need to protect the freedom of speech we have as Christians in America.

Take Action

> *You know that I have not hesitated to preach anything that would be helpful to you but have taught you publicly and from house to house.* (Acts 20:20 NIV).

Are We Fighting Where the Battle Rages?

1 – *Can you imagine saying something so offensive that when your audience hears it they try to kill you?*

> Jesus did just that. Reread the Gospels and the encounters Jesus had with leadership in and out of the church. Share

with your congregation what you discover about the messages Jesus preached.

2 – *Why is freedom of speech so important?*

Explain your answer.

3 – *What is the only law that should dictate what is said from the pulpit?*

Back up your answer.

4- *Should a church have to pay for their pastor to have freedom of speech?*

Why or why not?

5 – *What are the first and second clauses in the Bill of Rights?*

Why is it important that your congregation be made aware of these clauses and what they guarantee?

6 – *Given the respect the Bible accords to government, why has the church shied away from politics?*

7 – *Based on what you have learned about the founding documents of our government, should the IRS be allowed to violate the Constitution by demanding that a church give up its tax-exempt status because their pastor exercises his First Amendment rights of free speech and free religion from his pulpit? Do IRS rules trump the Constitution and the First Amendment?*

Explain your answers.

8 – *As American citizens, what mindset must Christians develop concerning absolute truth in regard to government, finance, business, the arts, religion, culture, education, media, and politics?*

Justify your answers.

Additional Resource Material

Pearcey, Nancy; Phillip E. Johnson (2008-03-31). "Total Truth: Liberating Christianity from Its Cultural Captivity" (Kindle Locations 964-969). Good News Publishers/Crossway Books. Kindle Edition.

"The Ten Commandments, Foundation of American Society" by Tony Perkins, Family Research Council

Section Three:

Solutions – What Are We Going to do About it?

Chapter 7

Pulpit Initiative – The Responsibility Is Ours

The issue of pastors preaching about politics from the pulpit is similar to the gifts of the Holy Spirit. Here is how most of the American body of Christ has **NOT** attained the whole measure of the fullness of Christ as Ephesians 4 says we should. Most of the Body of Christ does not accept the prophet as a viable gifting to the body to build it up as Ephesians 4:12 says, "to prepare God's people for works of service, so that the body of Christ may be built up until we all reach unity in the faith and in the knowledge of the Son of God and become mature, attaining to the whole measure of the fullness of Christ" (NIV).

Even though the Bible says in 1 Corinthians 12:1, "Now about spiritual gifts, brothers, I do not want you to be ignorant." There is still much ignorance among American Christians because I Corinthians 14:5 says, "I would like every one of you to speak in tongues…"

Now why are we not giving God what He likes? I mean is He God or are we? Do we tell God that this is how I want to serve You, or do we look to Scripture to find out what He likes and do what He likes?

Most of the American body of Christ not only doesn't speak in tongues, but also have never been prophesied over by a prophet even though 1 Corinthians 14:1 says, "Eagerly desire spiritual gifts, especially the gift of prophecy." Well, like prophecy and tongues, most of the body of Christ does not want to hear a political message from their pastor. Many believe that political things are on one side and spiritual things are on the other side, and we shouldn't mix the two.

The reason I have put politics and spiritual gifts together is that we are uniquely positioned to influence both greatly. I believe the Lord wants us to be ready to defend the belief that the gifts of the Spirit are for today, and that a timely message from a pastor about today's politics, is also for today.

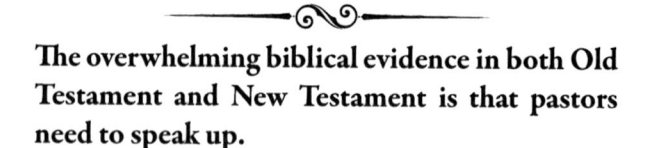

> **The overwhelming biblical evidence in both Old Testament and New Testament is that pastors need to speak up.**

Serving the Kingdom of God

The normal thing for a pastor to do before 1954 (the year religious free speech was attacked) with regard to politics was to give an election sermon concerning every election. Now the normal thing is to not get involved because his calling is about the kingdom of God and not the kingdom of man. There has been a fundamental shift in American theology that asks: "Mr. Pastor, why are you being so political?"

I have looked, but I don't see that when God asked Nathan (spiritual leader) to confront King David (political leader) of Israel concerning his immorality, Nathan said to God that it was too political, and he didn't want to get involved.

2 Samuel 12:1 says, "The Lord sent Nathan to David" (NIV). All throughout the Old Testament, God sent prophets and pastors to political leaders including Samuel, Elijah, Jeremiah, and Isaiah to name a few. So the feeling today is apparently now the Lord has changed His mind and doesn't want to mix the kingdom of God with the kingdom of man? Do we really think that is God's position on this? Certainly not.

I say that emphatically because hell is what is advanced when pastors remain silent about the moral issues of the day. It seems to me that much of an Old Testament leader's job was to confront wicked political leaders. Yet today the American spiritual leaders have taken what they feel is the high road and purposely not gotten involved in the low road of corrupt politics.

Many of my contemporaries actually come to me and say, "But Pastor Gus, we live in the New Testament and Jesus said in John 18:36, 'My kingdom is not of this world.' So if we get involved in politics, we are getting involved in the kingdom of man, and we are not involved in the kingdom of God!" This appears to be the theology about politics today.

They seem to be ignorant of not only the Old Testament example of the church leaders engaging politicians but also the New Testament examples as well. John the Baptist was killed for preaching publically about the private life of Governor Herod. But I guess to be fair; John the Baptist was actually an Old Testament prophet even though his story unfolds in the New Testament. However, you can go right down the line with church leaders like Peter, John, and Stephen of the New Testament church who confronted politicians throughout the book of Acts.

The overwhelming biblical evidence both Old Testament and New Testament is that pastors need to speak up. We need to start demanding true leadership from our politicians. In fact, to answer the question of why our nation is so morally bankrupt is to say it is the church's fault, especially the church leader's fault. The only way a man like Barack Obama could get elected is because the moral leaders of our churches are not leading their congregations in the moral issues.

Just like the Apostle Paul fought for his rights, pastors today need to fight for theirs as well. In Acts 16:35-39 we have read how the Apostle Paul's civil rights were violated. In 1954 this country began to violate the rights of pastors to freely preach the gospel concerning the moral issues of the day.

In Acts 22:22-29 Paul learned to use his rights and sets an example for pastors today. In Acts 23:27 the government protected Paul's rights, and we have those in our government today that will stand and fight for the rights of pastors who will challenge the unconstitutionality of the Johnson Amendment.

In order for our First Amendment freedom of speech to be protected, we, like Paul, must stand trial before Caesar or in our modern day language, have our day in court (Acts 27:24).

What Did Jesus Do?

Just like Jesus and His disciples were in the minority with their culture's spiritual leaders, we are too. So what do we do? Let's do what Jesus and His disciples did. They preached the truth and did not deviate from it. There is one scripture that is often used to deny spiritual gifts are being given by God in our day and age and one to keep politics out of the pulpits in America.

They use 1 Corinthians 13:10 which says, "When perfection comes, then the imperfect disappears." They believe that perfection is the word of God, but the context of the entire chapter is the people of God. So "perfection" is referring to the people of God not the word of God (Matthew 5:48, Hebrews 10:14, Hebrews 12:23).

John 18:36 is often used to explain why we should not engage in politics from the pulpit. The truth is when Jesus said His kingdom is not of this world it was neither an endorsement nor an exemption of engaging in politics. It is really just a statement that Christ's kingdom transcends this world. Jesus also said we are to be salt and light in every area of our world, even in politics.

Here is a modern-day example of the people of God influencing politics. Our brothers and sisters in the state of California voted on Proposition 8 which defines marriage as one man and one woman. They needed half of the total number of votes cast for Governor in the last election just to get it on the ballot. Proposition 22 (a law enacted by California voters in March of 2000 to restrict marriage to opposite sex partners) passed by 63 percent in 1999 and Proposition 8 passed by a margin of only 1.5 percent in 2008. If the church would have not gone on the offensive, marriage would not have been protected in California. Of course, they have now been struck down by the courts. Hosea 8:4 says, "They set up kings without my consent, they chose princes without my approval." This scripture defines the political mindset of the American church today. How sad is that? God always wants the godly to govern His people.

Charles Finney, one of the greatest revivalist preachers of American history said, "If there is a decay in conscience, the pulpit is responsible for it. If the public press lacks moral discernment, the pulpit is responsible for it. If the world loses its interest in Christianity, the pulpit is responsible for it. If satan rules in our halls of legislation, the pulpit is responsible for it. If our politics become so corrupt that the very foundations of our government are ready to fall away, the pulpit is responsible for it."

> **We need to be willing to sound the alarm from our pulpits and take a stand to defend faith, family, and freedom.**

Defend Our Rights, Declare the Truth, and Defeat the Enemy

We need to defend a pastor's right to speak about the moral issues of the day from his pulpit. We need to all watch what is going on in the culture around us. We need to pray individually and corporately for the wisdom to engage it biblically, courageously, and winsomely. We need to be willing to sound the alarm from our pulpits and take a stand to defend faith, family, and freedom.

We need to preach the Bible without apology on the moral issues that are being debated in the public arena today. We need to lead the church by calling for moral renewal in the culture and righteousness in our government. Paul tells Timothy, "I urge, then, first of all, that requests, prayers, intercession, and thanksgiving be made for everyone—for kings and all those in authority." One of the things on God's heart is government or "Kings" because when government functions the way God intended it to, His people can "lead quiet and peaceful lives in all godliness," and carry out God's Great Commission so that everyone has an opportunity "to be saved and to come to a knowledge of the truth" (1 Timothy 2:1-4).

We need to preach the clear standards of God in every area of our lives, like human life is precious in the sight of God and should be protected in public policy, and that sexual intimacy is reserved for one man and one woman in a covenant of marriage. When men try to silence us and take away our freedom to express our faith and truths of God's Word openly and publically, we need to stand fast in the liberty in which Christ has made us free!

Paul told the Ephesian leaders in Acts 20:27 to preach the whole counsel of God to the people of God and apply it to the moral issues of the day. Let us stand with the prophets and apostles of old like Moses who petitioned Pharaoh for the liberty of God's people, Elijah who faced off against King Ahab, Isaiah who condemned moral decay in the culture of his day, John the Baptist who publically pointed out Herod's adultery, and Peter who refused to bow down to the Jewish leadership who told him to stop preaching publically about Jesus. Let us declare with Peter, "We must obey God rather than men!"

> **When men try to silence us and take away our freedom to express our faith and truths of God's Word openly and publically, we need to stand fast in the liberty in which Christ has made us free!**

If there is any hope for America today, it is with the passionate praying of God's people and the prophetic preaching of God's pastors. Given all that is happening in our nation today, with human life becoming disposable, marriage being radically redefined, and our religious liberties being removed, we are faced with a hard choice. Will we rise up, stand up and speak up or will we sit down, submit, and surrender? Make no mistake, however, the battle we fight is not a military battle, it is not even a political battle, and it is not a cultural battle, it is a spiritual battle. To the victor goes the prize which is the America our children and grandchildren will inherit. That inheritance is based on what we do today in our generation. This point alone makes the consequences too alarming for me to just sit back, do nothing, and just watch it all happen.

This article from Pulpit Initiative speaks directly to what we can do:

Speaking Truth to the Culture *(July 9, 2013)*

> Recently, almost 1,600 churches from all fifty states took part in Pulpit Freedom Sunday. On June 9, 2013 pastors in these churches preached sermons about the importance of traditional marriage and to set forth what God says about marriage. This was the sixth annual Pulpit Freedom Sunday.

It began in 2008 as a direct challenge to the Johnson Amendment, a 1954 addition to the tax code that prohibits pastors from preaching freely on the issue of candidates and elections. Every year pastors participating in Pulpit Freedom Sunday have preached sermons that evaluated the candidates running for office in light of Scripture and made recommendations to their congregation as to how they ought to exercise their right to vote. The pastors recorded their sermons and sent them to the IRS in hopes of sparking a legal challenge to the Johnson Amendment. To date, not one of the over 1,600 pastors who have participated in Pulpit Freedom Sunday has been investigated by the IRS or punished for their sermons.

Because of the lack of national elections this year, pastors were encouraged to preach about the importance of marriage. That issue is front and center in light of the Supreme Court's decisions on marriage in June. Put simply, before the Supreme Court had its say about marriage, the Church had its say about how God designed marriage and intended for it to function.

Now that the Supreme Court has decided the marriage cases, what was decided? It is clear the battle over same-sex "marriage" will continue and the voice of America's pastors is even more necessary. If you are a pastor and did not get the opportunity to participate in Pulpit Freedom Sunday, now would be a great time to sign up. If you need resources on how to prepare a sermon on the issue, please visit our website. Taking part in Pulpit Freedom Sunday is a perfect opportunity to educate your congregation about marriage and why it should be protected as God intended. The responsibility is ours!

Pulpit Initiative Sunday sponsored by the ADF is your opportunity each year to speak up for freedom of speech in the church. Take the pulpit initiative!

Take Action

You know that I have not hesitated to preach anything that would be helpful to you but have taught you publicly and from house to house. (Acts 20:20 NIV).

Are We Taking Our Responsibility Seriously?

Go through this checklist and see what you have been doing and what you need to begin to do to take responsibility for the America our children and grandchildren will inherit!

- ___ I am sounding the alarm from my pulpit and taking a stand to defend faith, family, and freedom.
- ___ I am defending our rights, declaring the truth, and defeating the enemy.
- ___ I am preaching the Bible without apology on the moral issues that are being debated in the public arena today.
- ___ I am calling for moral renewal in the culture and righteousness in our government.
- ___ I am defending a pastor's right to speak about the moral issues of the day from his pulpit.
- ___ I am watching what is going on in the culture around us.
- ___ I am praying individually and corporately for the wisdom to engage these issues biblically, courageously, and winsomely.
- ___ I am preaching the clear standards of God in every area of our lives.
- ___ I am preaching the whole counsel of God to the people of God and apply it to the moral issues of the day.
- ___ I will rise up, stand up, and speak up whenever it is needed.

Additional Resource Material

Public Initiative Sunday information: http://www.adfmedia.org/news/prdetail/4360

Chapter 8

Pulpit Initiative vs. Complacency

Do you and your colleagues, friends, family, and church members believe that the Bible gives us principles to live by for every area of our lives? Some would argue that the Bible does not specifically say I should work at this job or that job or marry this person or that person. However, the Bible does give us principles to clearly discern the difference between working as a marijuana farmer or a soy bean farmer. It also clearly states that if I want to be married, I must choose someone from the opposite sex.

So the question is, "Would we be good stewards of God's Word if we were to allow those that wanted to marry a person of the same sex to do so or say we did not want to become involved in the politics of it?"

Some would argue that the Declaration of Independence has enshrined the fact that "all men are created equal, and they are endowed by their Creator with certain unalienable rights, that among them are life, liberty, and the pursuit of happiness." So if we preach against same-sex marriage, we are sticking our noses in where they don't belong and interfering with this particular group of people's happiness. After all, don't they have a right to be happy? Why should we interfere with their happiness?

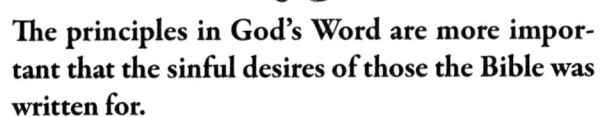

The principles in God's Word are more important that the sinful desires of those the Bible was written for.

God's Principles

There are many Christians that have issues with God's principles as they are set down in the Bible. Divorce is another area of concern. This was a problem even during Jesus' day. Matthew 19:3-9 gives us an example of what the religious leaders were dealing with in this area of divorce and what Jesus had to say about it. As you read this passage of scripture, think about the stand Jesus took, and whether or not He was confrontational or complacent.

> *Some Pharisees came to him to test him. They asked, "Is it lawful for a man to divorce his wife for any and every reason?"*
>
> *"Haven't you read," he replied, "that at the beginning the Creator 'made them male and female,' and said, 'For this reason a man will leave his father and mother and be united to his wife, and the two will become one flesh'? So they are no longer two, but one flesh. Therefore what God has joined together, let no one separate."*
>
> *"Why then," they asked, "did Moses command that a man give his wife a certificate of divorce and send her away?"*
>
> *Jesus replied, "Moses permitted you to divorce your wives because your hearts were hard. But it was not this way from the beginning. ⁹ I tell you that anyone who divorces his wife, except for sexual immorality, and marries another woman commits adultery."* (NIV)

Many people want a divorce today because they say they are married to the wrong person. Now-a-days people even get divorced saying they married the wrong sex. Did Jesus say that God's grace would cover this, and they should just go and be happy? Did He say, "That's all right, it's the way I created you so just go and be free and true to who you are"?

First of all, in verse four Jesus said God made them male and female and the two are to become united as husband and wife to become one flesh. We usually use this verse to preach against divorce, but it is also very clear concerning God's definition of marriage—one man and one woman. Note verse seven says, "Why then," they asked, "Did Moses command that **a man give his wife** a certificate of divorce and **send her away?**" Jesus said it was a **man** that gives his wife the divorce papers and then sends **her** away. Obviously this man was married to a woman. Jesus didn't even mention the possibility of marrying a person of the same sex.

In fact, the Holy Spirit has given us a list of wicked acts that those who commit them will not inherit the kingdom of God.

> *Or do you not know that wrongdoers will not inherit the kingdom of God? Do not be deceived: Neither the sexually immoral nor idolaters nor adulterers nor men who have sex with men nor thieves nor the greedy nor drunkards nor slanderers nor swindlers will inherit the kingdom of God. And that is what some of you were. But you were washed, you were sanctified, you were justified in the name of the Lord Jesus Christ and by the Spirit of our God.* (1 Corinthians 6:9-11 NIV)

The words *men who have sex with men* translate two Greek words that refer to the passive and active participants in homosexual acts. Several other translations of the Bible read "practice homosexuality" when translating this verse.

"Do not be deceived" means that if what is on this list is in your life and you still think you will inherit the kingdom of God, then you are deceived. I would like to point out that there are only a small percentage of people who deal with homosexuality in contrast to those who deal with the other wicked things on this list. Consider carefully everything on this list and realize the severity of the punishment for those who engage in **any** of them.

We also need to realize this list is not multiple choice. You can't say that because you don't do all of them you can still inherit the kingdom of God. If you do any of them, you will lose your inheritance. Those who get drunk or gossip or slander others or are greedy won't inherit the kingdom of God right along with those who practice homosexuality. Really? The greedy? Yes, and an example of possible greed is not giving back to God as instructed by the Bible, you are stealing from Him. Malachi 3:8 says, "Will a man rob God? Yet you rob me. But you ask, 'How do we rob you?'

In tithes and offerings." (NIV) If you do not tithe, you are a thief. In fact as you read further in Malachi you will see it deals directly with greed and idolatry as well (verse 9-10).

Many people believe the homosexual offender has a greater degree of wickedness than the greedy, idolatrous, thief but that is not what the scripture says. However, the Bible also makes provision for any and all sin. We can receive forgiveness through Jesus when we repent.

Romans 1:18-32 is titled *God's Wrath Against Mankind* in the New International Version Bible translation. Contained within these verses is a litany of wickedness that will incite God's wrath against us. Verses 26-27 specifically deal with the sin of homosexuality. The wickedness that is listed in verses 29-30 is explained in verse 28 which says, "Furthermore, since they did not think it worthwhile to retain the knowledge of God, he gave them over to a depraved mind, to do what ought not to be done."

God wants us to deal with these issues in our own lives but also says we are not to approve of those who practice these wicked acts (verse 32).

I can speak the truth of God's Word and openly declare and confront these issues:

"I do not approve of not tithing."
"I do not approve of slander or gossip."
"I do not approve of envy and greed."
"I do not approve of homosexuality."

However, if I decide to sit back and do nothing, if I am complacent about any of these issues, I am in fact making my approval of these wicked acts known. My lack of involvement actually indicates my approval.

Jesus said we are to be the light of the world because light exposes darkness. Would you ever vote to elect someone who wants to make stealing legal? You might if you intended to become a thief, but the problem then becomes legal for someone to now steal your stuff, too. I believe it is the same principle that involves voting for those we know are pro-abortion and want to legalize same-sex marriage. God has given us the ability to elect those who are going to make righteous laws based on God's principles or unrighteous laws which are in direct conflict with how God has instructed us to live.

Anyone who does not apply all of God's principles to all areas of their lives are in violation of God's law and will bring His wrath down upon themselves. So I ask again, "Do you believe the Bible gives us principles to live by for every area of our lives?"

So then the Bible is political because it wouldn't define righteous and unrighteous acts if it wasn't.

> *Righteousness exalts a nation, but sin condemns any people.*
> (Proverbs 14:34)

One of the ways righteousness can exalt this nation is when righteous people elect righteous people who make righteous laws.

Woe to You Who Are Complacent

Amos 6:1 says, "Woe to you who are complacent..."

Verse 6 says, "You do not grieve over the ruin of Joseph (meaning Israel or your country)." Do we grieve over the wicked laws in America?

Verse 7 says, "Therefore you will be among the first to go into exile." Exile is not being the strong nation they used to be. Is America as strong as she used to be?

Complacency played a part in Israel's ceasing to be a nation. The parallels and pitfalls of Old Testament Israel and New Testament America are incredible!

You can't blame the world for being worldly, so the complacency of the world is expected, but when our Bible warns Christians against wickedness and complacency and we still do nothing about it, is it any wonder that we are even still a nation? God does have wrath you know!

There is so much complacency, ignorance, and hostility in the body of Christ as to how the Bible applies itself to the electoral process of the Unites States of America that it doesn't surprise me in the least that our nation is going the way of Old Testament Israel. Is it crumbling into exile?

As a pastor I will always present some specific recommendations for my congregation as who to vote for. I will use the pulpit as a platform to endorse the candidacies that are the most biblically sound. I will evaluate their positions as well as the positions of their competitors through the lens of scripture and share with them what I have concluded. This is important because these will be the people who will be making decisions about what laws will govern this nation. Politicians are not perfect but some of them are more biblically principled than their competitors.

I told God over thirteen years ago when I started pastoring that He could count on me to tell them what they needed to hear, not only what they wanted to hear. What they need to hear and what this nation needs to hear, what your friends and relatives need to hear is that we must try to elect those who believe what the Bible teaches so our country does not go into exile.

We need to realize that America is exceptional in part because of its righteous laws. Did you know that during the time America has flourished under the Declaration of Independence, France has had fifteen different governments? We have had one since 1776. Brazil has had seven since 1822. Poland has had seven since 1921. Afghanistan has had five since 1923, and Russia has had four since 1918. This is the same in other nations of the world who have had various forms of government. Are there any other countries that have had one government as long as we have? Nope.

Foundationally, our laws were taken from the Bible, but our nation has deviated severely away from them. However, just like individuals can recant of their sins, our nation can as well. Remember Nineveh? Jonah was commanded to go to the pagan capital of the Assyrians and declare the truths of God and demand that they repent or be destroyed by God. At the obedience of one man God's wrath was averted. America needs many Christian leaders to have the courage of Jonah today.

Don't be complacent. Engage. Don't approve of those who practice evil by not voting for the most biblical candidates. Be a light. Be salt and preserve what God and our godly founders have given us. This is the most important issue of our generation! Be on the offensive: "The kingdom of heaven has been forcibly advancing and forceful men lay hold of it." (Matthew 11:12 NIV)

> *But the cowardly, the unbelieving, the vile, the murderers, the sexually immoral, those who practice magic arts, the idolaters and all liars—they will be consigned to the fiery lake of burning sulfur. This is the second death.* (Revelation 21:8 NIV)

Dare We Remain Silent?

Most of my pastoral peers are silent about taking the message of Christ into the realm of politics. One proof I have of that is the direction our laws are going and the lack of moral clarity of our legislators.

> *See how the faithful city has become a prostitute! She once was full of justice; righteousness used to dwell in her—but now murderers! Your silver has become dross, your choice wine is diluted with water. Your rulers are rebels, partners with thieves; they all love bribes and chase after gifts. They do not defend the cause of the fatherless; the widow's case does not come before them.*
>
> *Therefore the Lord, the LORD Almighty, the Mighty One of Israel, declares:*
>
> *"Ah! I will vent my wrath on my foes and avenge myself on my enemies. I will turn my hand against you; (the people) I will thoroughly purge away your dross and remove all your impurities."* (Isaiah 1:21-25 NIV)

God punished a nation because of its leaders.

> *Now here is the king you have chosen, the one you asked for; see, the LORD has set a king over you. If you fear the LORD and serve and obey him and do not rebel against his commands, and if both you and the king who reigns over you follow the LORD your God—good! But if you do not obey the LORD, and if you rebel against his commands, his hand will be against you, as it was against your ancestors.* (1 Samuel 12:13-15)

I don't want God's hand against me and my family but that is the reality if we "dare to remain silent."

When God's Word commands us in Exodus 18:21 to "select capable men...men who fear God, trustworthy men who hate dishonest gain and appoint them as your officials...." we as a nation are sinning if we do not do that or at least to try to do that. We as pastors have a responsibility to tell people who the most biblical candidates are. I believe it is a lack of leadership and a lack of courage for a pastor's theology about politics to be something like, "Well, I'll never tell my people who to vote for, but I will tell them they need to vote."

What if we had that theology with other areas of moral decision? If somebody came to you and wanted to cheat on his wife, would you not tell him what to do? My point is that if we can tell people who they are allowed to have sex with (only their spouse), we can certainly tell them who they should vote for.

Up until 1954 many congregations went to their pastors and asked, "Who is the most biblically qualified candidate?" After 1954 the tax code said non-profits cannot speak about politics without their tax exemption threatened to be revoked. Now the prevailing theology in the church is, "Don't tell me who to vote for." Too many pastors echo that sentiment which makes no sense to me.

We are the moral leaders of our communities, and how we cast our vote is a moral decision simply because there are moral implications at stake. Too many pastors have told me recently that they don't get political because they have people from both sides of the aisle in their church. That's like saying, "I don't preach against sin because I have both the righteous and the wicked in my congregation."

I personally came to the conclusion that I had to take a stand politically after reading the Democratic Party platform. When an understanding of how the Lord judges a nation by its laws and how He calls His leaders to confront it is realized, it is easy to conclude pastors sin by their "Switzerland Political Theology" (always neutral). I used to believe that for the sake of the gospel I shouldn't take sides politically. Now I believe **because** of the gospel I must take sides. I believe not taking a stand politically could very well be a sin.

John 7:13 says, "But no one would say anything publically about him (Jesus) for fear of the Jews." Today we can say pastors don't say things politically because of fear of the IRS or fear of offending the Democrats or Republicans. There is a stricter judgment for leaders in the body of Christ because to whom much is given much is required.

Let me also say as a balancing word, that the political realm is just part of the kingdom of God. It is not the kingdom of God. But to be involved in politics does not come at the expense of the gospel. The political realm and the church realm are not mutually exclusive. You have a right and a duty to tell people who the most biblically accurate candidate is and that constitutional right and biblical duty extends to your pulpit. You don't lose your First Amendment freedom of speech right when you step behind your pulpit, and you don't have to pay for that right either.

The separation between church and state argument comparison:

- Acts 16:35-39. Paul's rights were violated; *1954 our rights were violated.*
- Acts 22:22-29. Paul learned to use his rights; *2008 we learned to use our rights.*
- Acts 22:27. Because Paul stood up for his rights he wound up having those rights protected, *the same thing can happen to a pastor's right to say what he wants to from his pulpit without fear of punishment.*

The culmination of Paul's rights being violated resulted in an angel of the Lord saying to him in Acts 27:24, "Do not be afraid, Paul. You must stand trial before Caesar." That is so applicable for us today. We as pastors have gotten into this mess because of a lack of leadership and courage with some bad theology mixed in. People sometimes look at me and say I have youthful ignorance or selfish ambition, but I leave you with these two last quotes:

Dr. Martin Luther King, Jr. said, "Our lives begin to end the day we become silent about the things that matter." He broke an unrighteous law in order to make the law righteous (e.g., Rosa Parks).

Martin Luther said, "If I profess with the loudest voice and clearest exposition every portion of the truth of God except precisely that little point which the world and the devil are at the moment attacking, I am not confessing Christ. Where the battle rages there the loyalty of the soldier is proved."

There is a battle raging for the pulpits of America, and I question your loyalty if you dare to remain silent.

Take Action

> *You know that I have not hesitated to preach anything that would be helpful to you but have taught you publicly and from house to house.* (Acts 20:20 NIV).

Are We Complacent?

1 – *Do you and your colleagues, friends, family, and church members believe that the Bible gives us principles to live by for every area of our lives?*

   Explain your answer.

2 – *Would we be good stewards of God's Word if we were to allow those that wanted to marry a person of the same sex to do so or say we did not want to become involved in the politics of it?*

   Explain your answer.

3 – *Was Jesus confrontational or complacent concerning the issues of His day?*

   Read Matthew 19:3-9. As you read this passage of scripture, think about the stand Jesus took and whether or not He was confrontational or complacent.

4 – *Can you afford to be complacent about the things the Holy Spirit says are wicked and will keep people from inheriting the kingdom of God* (see Romans 1:18-32 *God's Wrath Against Mankind*)?

5 – *If you decide to sit back and do nothing, if you are complacent about any of these issues, do you realize you are in fact making your approval of these wicked acts known? Is that how you want the next generation to remember you and your ministry?*

6 – *What part did complacency play in Israel's ceasing to be a nation? What are the parallels and pitfalls of Old Testament Israel and New Testament America?*

7 – *Will you join me in saying,* "I will use the pulpit as a platform to endorse the candidacies that are the most biblically sound. I will evaluate their positions as well as the positions of their competitors through the lens of scripture and share with my congregation what I have concluded. I know this is important because these will be the people who will be making decisions about what laws will govern this nation. I will not be complacent; I will engage. I will not show my approval of those who practice evil by voting for them. I will be a light. I will be salt and preserve what God and our godly founders have given us. I will go on the offensive knowing religious free speech is the most important issue of our generation!"

Additional Resource Material

Please take advantage of all the resources I have given in the appendixes at the end of this book.

Final Word

I understand that this book's message is not a message where you feel encouraged in your personal life. You just need to know that the selfish will of almost any preacher wants to preach grace and love. They just want to preach things so that when they get done people feel like that was wonderful and say thank you. But that is the selfish will. When people say good job in any area, it makes you feel better. But when you know you have a message that isn't going to appeal to your selfish will or mine, it just stinks. Nonetheless it has got to be said. I have preached this material to my congregation, and I urge pastors to use this book as a resource for preaching the gospel about every area of Christian life to their congregants.

I am reminded of the real symbol of Christianity, the cross. The cross is not a feel good symbol just as this message is not a "feel your best about life" message. I can guarantee you no matter how perfect Jesus was, when He was hanging on the cross He wasn't thinking, "This is awesome. I love this. It is like the best day of my life." He was in tremendous pain and even said, "Why have You forsaken Me?" But when it was all said and done, I bet you He felt good that He had done what it was God the Father wanted Him to do. He was thankful that God used Him in a way that changed the world. I believe that giving glory to God as Jesus did on the cross and being thankful to Him are essentially the keys to not having a degrading culture. This is the part of the book where it is going to get personal in a good way.

If America would have stayed committed to the absolute truths of Scripture, given glory to God, and remained thankful to God through its history (as it started), I would have never needed to write a book like this. Can you imagine what it would be like if all of us were giving glory to

God with each one of our actions and each one of our lives and were being thankful for what God has given us?

We see in Romans 1:21-28 that the people of Paul's day in their thinking "became futile, their hearts were darkened, they became fools, and they exchanged God for images." All this happened because they were not giving glory to God and being thankful to God. That is paramount.

Instead of looking at this as a national problem, we need to look at it as an individual problem. If you look at it as an individual problem, all the national problems just go away. What is the greatest way each of us personally can glorify God? Simply do what He has called you to do. Just do what He has created you to do. That is it. That is the greatest way to glorify God. What's the simplest way to be thankful to God? It is to be happy in doing what He has created you to do.

When I first became a pastor, I did not want to become a pastor. I wanted to be a missionary. Well, I got my life right with God, and now I have accepted the calling on my life to be what it is He created me to be. That is not just true for those who are called to vocational ministry; it is true of every single human being. We are all to be and to do what it is we were created to do. If you don't know what it is, you might possibly stumble upon it through the grace of God, but wouldn't it just be so much easier to take a spiritual gifts questionnaire and discover this is what you were created to do?[60]

Some of you will find that what you were created to do becomes your vocation. That happened with me, but it is not true with everybody. Because you are gifted to do something, then do it whatever it is. If your gift is hospitality, you could be the one who brings in food every Friday for your office instead of saying, "Well they are just a bunch of sinners, why should I do that?" So be thankful for what God created you to do. I became thankful for my calling only a few years ago. I am not endeavoring to try and be a missionary anymore.

We need to be able to preach the full counsel of the Word of God. The full counsel of the word of God is being attacked. We need to realize we are getting attacked, and we need to rise up and do something about it. We need to be part of changing history. I believe God wants us to dream big

---

[60.] One free spiritual gifts survey is available at: http://www.churchgrowth.org/cgi-cg/gifts.cgi?intro=1

and shoot for everything that God has called us to do. We need to have that ambition.

That is the pinnacle of what God really wants us to understand. We are not called to be a "political" church. We are not called to be a "holier-than-thou church." We are called to be a church known as a loving church. We are called to be the church that is doing something that is needed to be done in our own community. We need to be interactive with others who need something from God. We need to be willing to get sloshed on the side of the road on our way to church by helping somebody out whose car has broken down. Loving people and being non-political is not an option.

So the message here is simple: *If we lose freedom of speech in the Church to speak the truth of the Gospel to every social, political, and cultural issue facing us, then we have lost the right to free speech in America that our founding documents and fathers fought so hard for. We must be bold and courageous in standing against the Johnson Amendment, the government institutions such as the IRS which seek to shut down free speech in the Church, and the politicians who would rob our culture of Christian moral and ethical standards. Will you be bold? Will you fight for righteousness and freedom of speech?*

Epilogue

Repealing the Johnson Amendment

At the writing of this book there is a bill that was introduced in the House called: H.R.127 – To restore the Free Speech and First Amendment rights of churches and exempt organizations by repealing the 1954 Johnson Amendment (113th Congress 2013-2014). Rep. Jones, Walter B. Jr. (R-NC-3) introduced it on 01/03/2013 with nineteen cosponsors. It has been referred to the House Committee on Ways and Means. Summary of this bill: "Amends the Internal Revenue Code to repeal the prohibition against churches and other tax-exempt organizations participating in political campaigns or supporting or opposing candidates for public office. Provides that this repeal shall not invalidate or limit any provision of the Federal Election Campaign Act of 1971."

Rep. Michele Bachmann (R-MN-6): "Repeal the Johnson Amendment" posted March 12, 2010. Americans United for Separation of Church and State, a radical leftist organization bent on intimidating pastors and churches into silence is making noise about a recent radio appearance by Rep. Michele Bachmann. Rep. Bachmann came right out and said what many pastors believe when she stated that Congress should repeal the Johnson Amendment. The Minnesota Independent reported Rep. Bachmann as saying, "The reason why clergy are afraid to be involved is because of an amendment that former President Lyndon Johnson passed when he was a senator from Texas…that stops 501(c)(3) organizations from saying anything political from the pulpit. Now, churches can be political from the pulpit. They can talk about issues all they want. What they can't do is endorse a candidate from the pulpit. But the ACLU has been all over the backs of churches...Christian and Jews and people of faith are not second class citizens...but these radical leftist organizations have been intimidating Christians for so long and pastors don't generally know that they do have the right to speak out from the pulpit. Congress should repeal that amendment from Lyndon Johnson...We need to repeal that and give Christians back their First Amendment rights to free speech in the church."

Pastor's Section

A Roadmap for Pastors

What do I need to do to protect my church?

"We receive many questions about what proactive steps churches can take to protect their religious liberty And with the recent Supreme Court decisions, this issue has taken center stage. Therefore, we have assembled a couple of resources all churches can use to best position themselves for the future.

First, read our resource *Seven Things all Churches Should have in their Bylaws*. We also have some suggested bylaw language on marriage and human sexuality that will help churches in this regard. Second, we advise every church to adopt a facilities usage policy that governs use of church facilities for wedding ceremonies. We have created a sample policy for you to use to ensure your church is protected.

Even in those states that adopted same-sex "marriage" or some equivalent, such as civil unions, churches do not have to allow use of their facilities for wedding ceremonies that are inconsistent with their faith. But there is an effort underway in some areas — such as Hawaii and Hutchinson, Kansas — to force churches to allow use of their facilities for same-sex "weddings" if they open their facilities for use by non-members for weddings at all. Passing a facilities usage policy provides a good defense. Put simply, no government official has the right to force a church to allow its facilities to be used for events that violate its religious beliefs.

Never forget that Alliance Defending Freedom is 'watching the legal horizon.' We will continue to keep you updated and provide the best ways you as a pastor can respond to protect your church from legal threats."[61]

A Roadmap for Pastors: Three Steps to Defend Biblical Truths

Posted on July 29th, 2013 by Nathan A. Cherry, The Family Policy Council of West Virginia

I've spent a lot of time with pastors encouraging them to get involved and be proactive in defending religious freedom, the sanctity of life, and marriage and family. Some are standing tall and speaking boldly. Some are sitting on the sidelines. And many others simply aren't so sure how to engage a culture that is moving steadily away from biblical truth.

One pastor recently asked me a simple question, "Where do I start?" He was feeling overwhelmed and just needed to know what the first step was in joining the conversation about the critical issues of the day. He also wanted guidance on how best to get his congregation informed and involved. That got me thinking about how many other pastors nationwide might be feeling the same.

Here is short list of steps every pastor can take to get started.

Step 1: Knowledge is Power: Stay informed on the critical issues.

As a pastor, your congregation needs to know they can come to you with questions and concerns about pressing social issues. They want you to engage in intelligent

---

[61] http://www.speakupmovement.org/Church/Content/userfiles/Resources/church_seven_bylaws.pdf

conversation and provide them with the biblical firepower to combat the half-truths and misconceptions perpetuated throughout society. Nothing is more frustrating or discouraging to a church member than to ask their pastor important questions on fundamental religious issues, only to receive vapid responses such as, "I don't pay attention to trivial things in society," or "Don't waste your time reading the news, just read the Bible."

But there is nothing trivial about the issues of religious liberty, life, and marriage and family. For many church attendees, the issues of life and marriage are central to their everyday lives, and they need to know their pastor can handle their questions. Nothing screams "irrelevant" like not having a clue about what is going on in society.

Tip: Use a good news aggregator to stay informed. I use *Feedly*. This way, instead of having to go to a dozen websites for news, the news will come to you. I recommend following the *Engage Family Minute*, Alliance Defending Freedom's *Alliance Alert* and *Speak Up Church Blog*, Family Research Council's *FRC Blog*, *World Net Daily*, and *Life News*. If you follow these, you will be well-informed.

Step 2: Spread the Knowledge: Share information with your congregation.

As a pastor, your congregation looks to you for guidance. A pastor can harness his influence to teach his flock a practical theology—a lived faith that stands tall against liberal trends that mock God's ways. If a pastor stays informed and shares this Godly information with his congregation, they will increasingly see him as someone they can trust and count on.

When major news happens, talk about it in church. If a pastor ignores crucial events like the Sandy Hook shooting or the Supreme Court rulings on marriage, he will be missing prime teaching opportunities that can bring biblical truths to light. There is more than just a social context to these events; there is an opportunity to share deep biblical truth about God's design for human dignity, life, and marriage. And once your congregation is equipped in this gospel knowledge, they will be able to share it with all who cross their path.

Tip: Use social media to teach even when you're not preaching. By using social media, you can have tremendous influence on your congregation even when they are not in church. Don't be afraid to share articles or comment on events happening in the community and around the country.

Step 3: Faith in Action: Encourage the flock to be informed and active.

A lot of pastor's want to steer clear of being "too political" in church. But even if this is the case, that doesn't mean a pastor can't encourage his congregation to stay informed and be active. Just because your church may not hold a pro-life rally, that doesn't mean you can't encourage others to participate in one elsewhere. Many worthwhile national events like the Sanctity of Human Life Sunday, Pulpit Freedom Sunday, National Day of Prayer, and Call 2 Fall provide an excellent opportunity to unite your congregation in a lived faith that sets an example for the community. You can't simply say you are pro-life or pro-marriage without getting involved. Faith demands action.

By staying informed on local and national events, you can encourage your congregation to be an active light in the community and stand for biblical truth. This can only lead to infinite opportunities to spread the gospel.

Tip: Set an example for your congregation by personally getting involved. You can do this by letting your church know you are voting and encouraging them to do the same. You can also support a local, state, or national organization as a church and work as a community to bring about lasting change. Organizations like Care Pregnancy Centers can never have enough support. Take action and encourage others to do the same.

These are just three small steps that a pastor can take to advance the gospel and lead others in standing for God's truth. If a pastor does not care about biblical issues being assaulted in society, why should their congregation?

It is only once a pastor is armed with knowledge and the will to share and act on it that others will follow. And maybe once this happens, Christians across America will be able to help prevent and overturn bad court decisions such as *Roe v. Wade* or the striking down of one of the crucial articles of DOMA defining marriage as the union of one man and one woman. There are no short-cuts. Our nation's spiritual leaders must rise to the occasion so that others may follow to preserve religious liberty, life, marriage and family.

© 2013 Alliance Defending Freedom. All Rights Reserved. Use by permission.

Appendix 1

Keep Your Beliefs to Yourself

Examples of Government Violating the Biblical View of Marriage
Published by MINNESOTA Family Council 8.1.2013

As we're sure you remember, just last year one man–one woman marriage supporters were told often and loudly "not to worry," that there was "no real threat to marriage."

Now, only months later, Minnesotans face August 1, 2013—the day when gay "marriages" will begin in Minnesota after proponents successfully spent over $2 Million to convince the Minnesota Legislature to force gay "marriage" on the state. Turns out there was a threat to Marriage after all.

Gay "marriage" supporters are hailing August 1st as an historic day for their misguided view of what "equality" means, while over 1.4 Million Minnesotans who continue to believe in one man–one woman marriage recognize that a gender-neutral society is not good for anyone (especially children) and that our state will be facing the consequences of what a few legislators forced on us for years to come—including a very clear and present threat to Minnesotans' right to religious liberty.

Big WHOPPER of the Year: "The Gay 'Marriage' Bill Protects Your Religious Liberties"

Last year, gay "marriage" supporters told us there was no threat to our traditional definition of marriage…and now gay "marriage" starts in

MINNESOTA on August 1ˢᵗ. This year, they are hailing the gay "marriage" bill as a colossal "win" for religious liberty.

This WHOPPER reveals three things:

1. Gay "marriage" supporters know that religious liberty is important to ALL Minnesotans so they knew they had to pretend that religious freedom would be protected in order to get the Legislature to force gay "marriage" on the state;

2. There is a grave misunderstanding and lack of respect for people of faith by gay "marriage" proponents; AND

3. The real bigotry is against people with deeply held beliefs about what Marriage really is.

The result? Now over 1.4 million Minnesotans are considered the legal equivalent of "bigots" and have NO protection to live out their beliefs in the public square.

The gay "marriage" law allows churches and SOME religious organizations to define marriage as only between one man and one woman. But, people of faith know that living out your beliefs means living what you believe OUTSIDE the walls of your church.

Gay "marriage" supporters and their allies in the Minnesota Legislature seem to think that Minnesotans with deeply held religious beliefs about Marriage will be content to believe that marriage is the union of one man and one woman in the walls of their church and then stay SILENT about those beliefs outside those walls.

So, the Minnesota Legislature passed the gay "marriage" bill with no protections for people outside the walls of their church. The Minnesota Senate had the chance—and refused—to protect the religious liberty rights of Minnesotans outside their church walls.

Now Minnesotans with the deeply held belief that marriage is the union of one man and one woman cannot act on this belief in the way they do their business or the way they practice their profession.

The Minnesota Department of Human Rights has already confirmed our worst fears: There is NO religious liberty protection for people of faith in the public square.

The Department states specifically that nonreligious organizations are NOT exempt from the law and that nondiscrimination laws can (and will) be used as a weapon to punish people of faith. For example, if a Christian, Jewish, or Muslim florist refused to provide flowers for a same-sex "wedding" based on his religious beliefs, the same-sex couple can "file a claim with the Minnesota Department of Human Rights against the entity that discriminated against them."

Bottom Line? The gay "marriage" lobby and their allies in the Minnesota Legislature view Minnesotans of faith as "bigots" and will punish them accordingly using Minnesota Human Rights laws—forcing men and women of faith to choose between their livelihood and their convictions.

That is not acceptable.

We Know What's Coming...

Though it's impossible to know all the consequences of creating a genderless society by enacting gay "marriage," we do know one thing for sure: Like clockwork in states that already have gay "marriage" (or even states with only civil unions or other legal arrangements), **people who have deeply held beliefs that marriage is only the union of one man and one woman become marginalized and are punished as bigots by state laws. Over 1.4 Million Minnesotans could be impacted in this way.**

Here are just a FEW of the examples of states that are being violated by gay "marriage."

New York:

- New York town clerks resign rather than be forced to sign same-sex "marriage" licenses against their Christian beliefs.
- Robert & Cynthia, New York farm owners, face a discrimination complaint, including significant fines and penalties if found

in violation of the state's anti-discrimination laws, and potentially having to choose between their beliefs and operating their business.

New Mexico:

- Elaine Huguenin fined over $6,000 for discrimination when she refused to photograph a same-sex ceremony based on her religious beliefs.

Massachusetts:

- David & Tonia Parker were given no right to opt their kindergartner out of instruction on gay "marriage" or even get prior notice of such instruction—despite their religious beliefs.
- Jim & Mary O'Reilly, B&B owners, were sued for discrimination and forced to settle the case due to significant economic loss to their business after they refused to provide their services to a same-sex wedding because of their deeply held Catholic beliefs.

Colorado:

- Christian bakery owners face a discrimination complaint for refusing to make a cake for a same-sex ceremony—they may be punished with fines or even jail time!

Washington:

- Barronelle Stutzman, a florist for 30 years, faces a discrimination lawsuit by the ACLU and the State of Washington for refusing to do the flowers for a gay "wedding" based on her Christian beliefs.

D.C.:

- Catholic Charities shuts down adoption/foster care program due to same-sex "marriage" law.

We know this state-sanctioned discrimination is en route for Minnesota's men and women of faith—yet the vast majority of Americans (and Minnesotans) believe that religious liberty SHOULD be protected in the public square.

Defend Religious Liberties

The right to religious liberty should matter to ALL of us. If your deeply held beliefs are being threatened one day, it may be another's deeply held beliefs threatened the next.

Don't sit on the sidelines!

Don't sit by and let your beliefs be silenced. Deeply held religious beliefs are meant to be lived out—not hidden away in a dark corner of your church building!

> *"You are the salt of the earth; but if the salt loses its flavor, how shall it be seasoned? It is then good for nothing but to be thrown out and trampled underfoot by men. You are the light of the world. A city that is set on a hill cannot be hidden. Nor do they light a lamp and put it under a basket, but on a lampstand, and it gives light to all who are in the house. Let your light so shine before men, that they may see your good works and glorify your Father in heaven."* (Matthew 5:13-16)

Don't be silenced!

God bless you,

John Helmberger

(This letter was written by John Helmberger, CEO of the Minnesota Family Council.)

Appendix 2

A Sampling of Christian writings from our American Founding Fathers

Samuel Adams
Father of the American Revolution, Signer of the Declaration of Independence

I ... recommend my Soul to that Almighty Being who gave it, and my body I commit to the dust, relying upon the merits of Jesus Christ for a pardon of all my sins.

Will of Samuel Adams

Charles Carroll
Signer of the Declaration of Independence

On the mercy of my Redeemer I rely for salvation and on His merits; not on the works I have done in obedience to His precepts.

From an autographed letter in our possession written by Charles Carroll to Charles W. Wharton, Esq., on September 27, 1825, from Doughoragen, Maryland.

William Cushing
First Associate Justice Appointed by George Washington to the Supreme Court

Sensible of my mortality, but being of sound mind, after recommending my soul to Almighty God through the merits of my Redeemer and my body to the earth...

Will of William Cushing

John Dickinson
Signer of the Constitution

Rendering thanks to my Creator for my existence and station among His works, for my birth in a country enlightened by the Gospel and enjoying freedom, and for all His other kindnesses, to Him I resign myself, humbly confiding in His goodness and in His mercy through Jesus Christ for the events of eternity.

Will of John Dickinson

John Hancock
Signer of the Declaration of Independence

I John Hancock,... being advanced in years and being of perfect mind and memory-thanks be given to God-therefore calling to mind the mortality of my body and knowing it is appointed for all men once to die [Hebrews 9:27], do make and ordain this my last will and testament...Principally and first of all, I give and recommend my soul into the hands of God that gave it: and my body I recommend to the earth... nothing doubting but at the general resurrection I shall receive the same again by the mercy and power of God...

Will of John Hancock

Patrick Henry
Governor of Virginia, Patriot

This is all the inheritance I can give to my dear family. The religion of Christ can give them one which will make them rich indeed.

Will of Patrick Henry

John Jay
First Chief Justice of the US Supreme Court

Unto Him who is the author and giver of all good, I render sincere and humble thanks for His manifold and unmerited blessings, and especially for our redemption and salvation by His beloved son. He has been pleased to bless me with excellent parents, with a virtuous wife, and with worthy children. His protection has companied me through many eventful years, faithfully employed in the service of my country; His providence has not only conducted me to this tranquil situation but also given me abundant reason to be contented and thankful. Blessed be His holy name!

Will of John Jay

Daniel St. Thomas Jenifer
Signer of the Constitution

In the name of God, Amen. I, Daniel of Saint Thomas Jenifer . . . of dispossing mind and memory, commend my soul to my blessed Redeemer. . .

Will of Daniel St. Thomas Jenifer

Henry Knox
Revolutionary War General, Secretary of War

First, I think it proper to express my unshaken opinion of the immortality of my soul or mind; and to dedicate and devote the same to the supreme head of the Universe – to that great and tremendous Jehovah, – Who created the universal frame of nature, worlds, and systems in number infinite . . . To this awfully sublime Being do I resign my spirit with unlimited confidence of His mercy and protection . . .

Will of Henry Knox

John Langdon
Signer of the Constitution

In the name of God, Amen. I, John Langdon, . . . considering the uncertainty of life and that it is appointed unto all men once to die [Hebrews 9:27], do make, ordain and publish this my last will and testament in manner following, that is to say-First: I commend my soul to the infinite mercies of God in Christ Jesus, the beloved Son of the Father, who died and rose again that He might be the Lord of the dead and of the living . . . professing to believe and hope in the joyful Scripture doctrine of a resurrection to eternal life . . .

Will of John Langdon

John Morton
Signer of the Declaration of Independence

With an awful reverence to the great Almighty God, Creator of all mankind, I, John Morton . . . being sick and weak in body but of sound mind and memory-thanks be given to Almighty God for the same, for all His mercies and favors-and considering the certainty of death and the uncertainty of the times thereof, do, for the settling of such temporal estate as it hath pleased God to bless me with in this life . . .

Will of John Morton

Robert Treat Paine
Signer of the Declaration of Independence

I desire to bless and praise the name of God most high for appointing me my birth in a land of Gospel Light where the glorious tidings of a Savior and of pardon and salvation through Him have been continually sounding in mine ears.

Robert Treat Paine, *The Papers of Robert Treat Paine*, Stephen Riley and Edward Hanson, editors (Boston: Massachusetts Historical Society, 1992), Vol. I, p. 48, March/April, 1749.

[W]hen I consider that this instrument contemplates my departure from this life and all earthly enjoyments and my entrance on another state of existence, I am constrained to express my adoration of the Supreme Being, the Author of my existence, in full belief of his providential goodness and his forgiving mercy revealed to the world through Jesus Christ, through whom I hope for never ending happiness in a future state, acknowledging with grateful remembrance the happiness I have enjoyed in my passage through a long life...

Will of Robert Treat Paine

Charles Cotesworth Pinckney
Signer of the Constitution

To the eternal, immutable, and only true God be all honor and glory, now and forever, Amen!...

Will of Charles Cotesworth Pinckney

Rufus Putnam
Revolutionary War General, First Surveyor General of the United States

[F]irst, I give my soul to a holy, sovereign God Who gave it in humble hope of a blessed immortality through the atonement and righteousness of Jesus

Christ and the sanctifying grace of the Holy Spirit. My body I commit to the earth to be buried in a decent Christian manner. I fully believe that this body shall, by the mighty power of God, be raised to life at the last day; 'for this corruptable (sic) must put on incorruption and this mortal must put on immortality.' [I Corinthians 15:53]

Will of Rufus Putnam

Benjamin Rush
Signer of the Declaration of Independence

My only hope of salvation is in the infinite, transcendent love of God manifested to the world by the death of His Son upon the cross. Nothing but His blood will wash away my sins. I rely exclusively upon it. Come, Lord Jesus! Come quickly!

Benjamin Rush, *The Autobiography of Benjamin Rush*, George Corner, editor (Princeton: Princeton University Press for the American Philosophical Society, 1948), p. 166, Travels Through Life, An Account of Sundry Incidents & Events in the Life of Benjamin Rush.

Roger Sherman
Signer of the Declaration of Independence, Signer of the Constitution

I believe that there is one only living and true God, existing in three persons, the Father, the Son, and the Holy Ghost.... that the Scriptures of the Old and New Testaments are a revelation from God.... that God did send His own Son to become man, die in the room and stead of sinners, and thus to lay a foundation for the offer of pardon and salvation to all mankind so as all may be saved who are willing to accept the Gospel offer.

Lewis Henry Boutell, *The Life of Roger Sherman* (Chicago: A. C. McClurg and Company, 1896), pp. 272-273.

Richard Stockton
Signer of the Declaration of Independence

I think it proper here not only to subscribe to the entire belief of the great and leading doctrines of the Christian religion, such as the Being of God, the universal defection and depravity of human nature, the divinity of the person and the completeness of the redemption purchased by the blessed Savior, the necessity of the operations of the Divine Spirit, of Divine Faith, accompanied with an habitual virtuous life, and the universality of the divine Providence, but also . . . that the fear of God is the beginning of wisdom; that the way of life held up in the Christian system is calculated for the most complete happiness that can be enjoyed in this mortal state; that all occasions of vice and immorality is injurious either immediately or consequentially, even in this life; that as Almighty God hath not been pleased in the Holy Scriptures to prescribe any precise mode in which He is to be publicly worshiped, all contention about it generally arises from want of knowledge or want of virtue.

Will of Richard Stockton

Jonathan Trumbull Sr.
Governor of Connecticut, Patriot

Principally and first of all, I bequeath my soul to God the Creator and Giver thereof, and body to the Earth . . . nothing doubting but that I shall receive the same again at the General Resurrection thro the power of Almighty God; believing and hoping for eternal life thro the merits of my dear, exalted Redeemer Jesus Christ.

Will of Jonathan Trumbull

John Witherspoon
Signer of the Declaration of Independence

I entreat you in the most earnest manner to believe in Jesus Christ, for there is no salvation in any other [Acts 4:12]. . . . [I]f you are not reconciled to God through Jesus Christ, if you are not clothed with the spotless robe of His righteousness, you must forever perish.

John Witherspoon, *The Works of John Witherspoon* (Edinburgh: J. Ogle, 1815), Vol. V, pp. 276, 278, The Absolute Necessity of Salvation Through Christ, January 2, 1758.

(This information provided by Wallbuilders at: http://www.wallbuilders.com/libissuesarticles.asp?id=78)

Appendix 3

Two Letters from Pastor Gus Booth to Colleagues in Ministry

My Ministry Peers,

I am pastor of Warroad Community Church in Warroad, Minnesota—six miles from the Canadian border. I have always had a passion for preaching the Gospel, especially as it applies to society and government.

The Gospel is living and active and applies to all of life. One area in particular where the light of the Gospel has not been shined very brightly is the political realm. Pastors seem too hesitant to address the political realm these days with the truth of Scripture, instead preferring to turn a blind eye to corruption and evil in our national and local leaders. Many of the pastors I know refuse to address the political issues of the day and instead remain silent. Even though I felt strongly that I should be preaching what the Bible says about selecting the leaders of our country, I believed that it was illegal to say anything from the pulpit, especially about candidates and during an election cycle.

I feared what the IRS would do to my church if I said something I shouldn't. The last thing I, or any pastor for that matter, wants is an IRS audit.

That's why, in 2008, when I heard about ADF's Pulpit Initiative, I was immediately interested. I responded immediately to get more information and the more I looked into the Pulpit Initiative and talked with ADF's attorneys about the purpose of the Pulpit Initiative; I knew I had to be involved in the very first year of the Initiative. I signed up immediately, preached my sermon on Pulpit Freedom Sunday and sent my sermon to the IRS.

The Pulpit Initiative is long overdue. For too many years, pastors have conveniently hidden behind the idea that it is against the law to apply Scripture to elections and candidates. I see ADF as the offensive line protecting the pastoral quarterback who cannot successfully hand off to the next generation of running backs without the offensive line's help. And it's about time that we got on offense instead of sitting passively on the defensive while our right to speak freely from the pulpit is stripped away.

The IRS did audit my church and ADF was there every step of the way. Fighting the IRS was never a fearful event for me because I knew ADF was representing me. The IRS eventually dropped the audit for reasons of their own, but I continue to speak boldly from the pulpit–even about candidates and elections–because I know that it is the right thing to do and that ADF stands ready to defend any encroachment on my liberty as a pastor to freely proclaim God's word to my congregation on any and every issue.

ADF is prophetically calling the true leaders of America (pastors) out of the cave of hiding, much like the prophet Gad did with the true leader of Israel, King David. The Lord has an opinion on every moral issue, and His leaders need to give it. But it is much easier to give that opinion, knowing that ADF and its team of attorneys are standing behind and supporting pastors.

As the apostle Paul learned to use his rights as a Roman citizen to protect the gospel in the 1st century, the ADF is doing the same for us in the 21st. Their professionalism and commitment to the gospel is second to none, even when compared with many pastors. It is a sad day when the pulpit is more protected by attorneys than pastors. We pastors need to rise up and give the ADF something to protect.

In His Service,

Pastor Gustav L. Booth (Gus)

My Ministry Peers,

To not engage in the political process is to not allow the gospel of Jesus Christ into an arena that is desperate for His influence. You are a leader that needs to rise up and take a stand for Jesus even in areas that may offend your congregation.

Evaluate the candidates and make recommendations to your congregation as to who they should vote for. We, as Christian leaders, recommend to our congregations how to live in all areas of life. Why should politics be any different?

Does wickedness or righteousness "jump for joy" when the ungodly are elected? The only influence against wickedness is righteousness. So you being a minister of righteousness must take a stand.

Martin Luther once said, "If I profess with the loudest voice and clearest exposition every portion of the truth of God except precisely that little point which the world and the devil are at that moment attacking, I am not confessing Christ ... Where the battle rages there the loyalty of the soldier is proved." The battle is raging in the area of politics. Please, my co-laborer in Christ, I plead with you to engage.

"If there is a decay of conscience, the pulpit is responsible for it. If the public press lacks moral discernment, the pulpit is responsible for it. If the church is degenerate and worldly, the pulpit is responsible for it. If the world loses its interest in Christianity, the pulpit is responsible for it. If Satan rules in our halls of legislation, the pulpit is responsible for it. If our politics become so corrupt that the very foundations of our government are ready to fall away, the pulpit is responsible for it." Charles Finney

I have purposed in my heart that my pulpit will not be responsible for it. Have you?

In His Service,

Pastor Gustav L. Booth (Gus)

Appendix 4

Resources to Embolden You with the Facts

STEP BY STEP, "SMALL" CASES REGAIN LEGAL GROUND FOR THE GOSPEL!

By Alan Sears posted Aug 6, 2013

Sometimes, progress comes with what the world would call small steps.

It's easier, perhaps, when we're writing to you about Supreme Court cases, to understand the enormity of what's at stake for you and your family in our daily struggle to defend religious freedom in America. But most of the hundreds of cases that will decide your future come in smaller packages, with a lot less fanfare. They simply reflect the determination of people just like you to stand for Christ in their daily walk and personal circumstances, and our determination to defend their right to do that.

Consider, for instance, the young elementary school student in Temple Terrace, Florida, who wanted nothing more than to invite some of his fellow fourth graders to an Easter egg hunt in his neighborhood. He and his mother had organized the event to include games, snacks, candy, and a presentation of the Easter story. They prepared invitations and the boy took great care to hand them out during non-instructional time at school.

"No good," said the principal, explaining in a note sent home to the parents that students "are not allowed to pass out fliers related to religious events or activities." Yet, oddly, other children were given permission all the time to pass out invitations to birthday parties, Halloween festivities, soccer games, etc.

"Public schools should encourage, not shut down, the free exchange of ideas," says Legal Counsel Matt Sharp, who joined other Alliance Defending Freedom staff and allied attorneys in filing a lawsuit against the Hillsborough County School district on behalf of the student. "A ban on a simple invitation of this sort, offered from one student to another during non-instructional time, is disturbing and unconstitutional." In the wake of our lawsuit, a federal court struck down the district's policies last fall, and now the school has revised its code accordingly.

A change of policy was also in order for the East Baton Rouge (Louisiana) Recreation and Park Commission, which had banned a Sidewalk Sunday School sponsored by a local ministry.

Voices of Mercy Outreach Ministries had obtained permission from the commission to use a local park for its activities with at-risk youth living in the low income area way back in 2005. Five years into the program, though, the commission did an about-face, saying the outreach violated a policy that prohibits using the park for religious purposes. (Curiously, officials had allowed at least one other religious group to hold an event at the park).

Our attorneys filed suit on behalf of the program, and the commission recently agreed, as part of a settlement of that lawsuit, to amend its policy and allow the Sunday School to continue.

"Faith-based groups have the same constitutionally protected freedom as any other community group to hold activities at a public park," says Senior Legal Counsel Joel Oster. "We commend the commission for recognizing that such groups shouldn't be singled out for discrimination – especially a group like this that has provided such selfless service to at-risk youth and their parents for many years."

Small steps, perhaps, in the great scheme of things ... but crucial victories, as by God's grace we regain, step by step, the legal ground lost to those who would close public doors to the Gospel.

These are the victories that are subtly shaping what tomorrow will look like in the world where our children and grandchildren live out their lives and faith. Please join me in praying for our attorneys, and for all those standing firm – in cases "big" and "small" – for the right to live openly, gracefully, thoughtfully for Christ in their community. (http://blog.alliancedefendingfreedom.org/2013/08/06/step-by-step-small-cases-regain-legal-ground-for-the-gospel/)

Excerpts from the <u>Northern Colorado Gazette:</u> July 25, 2013

Using the same tactics used by "gay" rights activists, pedophiles have begun to seek similar status arguing their desire for children is a sexual orientation no different than heterosexual or homosexuals.

Critics of the homosexual lifestyle have long claimed that once it became acceptable to identify homosexuality as simply an "alternative lifestyle" or sexual orientation, logically nothing would be off limits. "Gay" advocates have taken offense at such a position insisting this would never happen. However, psychiatrists are now beginning to advocate redefining pedophilia in the same way homosexuality was redefined several years ago.

In 1973 the American Psychiatric Association declassified homosexuality from its list of mental disorders. A group of psychiatrists with B4U-Act recently held a symposium proposing a new definition of pedophilia in the Diagnostic and Statistical Manual of Mental Health Disorders of the APA.

B4U-Act calls pedophiles "minor-attracted people." The organization's website states its purpose is to, "help mental health professionals learn more about attraction to minors and to consider the effects of stereotyping, stigma and fear."

In 1998 the APA issued a report claiming "that the 'negative potential' of adult sex with children was 'overstated' and that 'the vast majority' of both men and women reported no negative sexual effects from childhood sexual abuse experiences."

Pedophilia has already been granted protected status by the Federal Government. The Matthew Shephard and James Byrd, Jr. Hate Crimes Prevention Act lists "sexual orientation" as a protected class; however, it does not define the term.

Republicans attempted to add an amendment specifying that "pedophilia is not covered as an orientation;" however, the amendment was defeated by Democrats. Rep. Alcee Hastings (D-Fl) stated that all alternative sexual lifestyles should be protected under the law. "This bill addresses our resolve to end violence based on prejudice and to guarantee that all Americans, regardless of race, color, religion, national origin, gender, sexual orientation, gender identity, or disability or all of these 'philias' and fetishes and 'isms' that were put forward need not live in fear because of who they are. I urge my colleagues to vote in favor of this rule." *(Please understand that this elected official just put the rights of an adult to have sex with a child above the rights of a child to not be sexually violated. Christians in that woman's district should make sure she never even sees the electable side of a ballot let alone actually get elected. -Gus Booth)*

The White House praised the bill saying, "At root, this isn't just about our laws; this is about who we are as a people. This is about whether we value one another – whether we embrace our differences rather than allowing them to become a source of animus." *(I read this to mean that certain government leaders are okay with children being raped! –Gus Booth)*

Earlier this year two psychologists in Canada declared that pedophilia is a sexual orientation just like homosexuality or heterosexuality.

Van Gijseghem, psychologist and retired professor of the University of Montreal, told members of Parliament, "Pedophiles are not simply people who commit a small offense from time to time but rather are grappling with what is equivalent to a sexual orientation just like another individual may be grappling with heterosexuality or even homosexuality."

He went on to say, "True pedophiles have an exclusive preference for children, which is the same as having a sexual orientation. You cannot change this person's sexual orientation. He may, however, remain abstinent."

When asked if he should be comparing pedophiles to homosexuals, Van Gijseghem replied, "If, for instance, you were living in a society where heterosexuality is proscribed or prohibited and you were told that you had to get therapy to change your sexual orientation, you would probably say that that is slightly crazy. In other words, you would not accept that at all. I use this analogy to say that, yes indeed, pedophiles do not change their sexual orientation." *(Well if they don't then let your child be the first to have sex with them, right? That was sarcasm. –Gus Booth)*

Dr. Quinsey, professor emeritus of psychology at Queen's University in Kingston, Ontario, agreed with Van Gijseghem. Quinsey said pedophiles' sexual interests prefer children and, "There is no evidence that this sort of preference can be changed through treatment or through anything else." *(So just because there is no evidence then let's not try to find any either. Quite frankly if you even need any evidence to prove adults having sex with children is detrimental to those children; you need your own head examined. – Gus Booth)*

In July, 2010 Harvard health Publications said, "Pedophilia is a sexual orientation and unlikely to change. Treatment aims to enable someone to resist acting on his sexual urges."

Linda Harvey, of Mission America, said the push for pedophiles to have equal rights will become more and more common as LGBT groups continue to assert themselves. "It's all part of a plan to introduce sex to children at younger and younger ages; to convince them that normal friendship is actually a sexual attraction."

Milton Diamond, a University of Hawaii professor and director of the Pacific Center for Sex and Society, stated that child pornography could be beneficial to society because, "Potential sex offenders use child pornography as a substitute for sex against children."

Diamond is a distinguished lecturer for the Institute for the Advanced Study of Human Sexuality in San Francisco. The IASHS openly advocated for the repeal of the Revolutionary war ban on homosexuals serving in the military.

The IASHS lists, on its website, a list of "basic sexual rights" that includes "the right to engage in sexual acts or activities of any kind whatsoever, providing they do not involve nonconsensual acts, violence, constraint, coercion or fraud." Another right is to, "be free of persecution, condemnation, discrimination, or societal intervention in private sexual behavior" and "the freedom of any sexual thought, fantasy or desire." The organization also says that no one should be "disadvantaged because of age." *(Scary! – Gus Booth)*

Sex offender laws protecting children have been challenged in several states including California, Georgia and Iowa. Sex offenders claim the laws prohibiting them from living near schools or parks are unfair because it penalizes them for life. (http://patdollard.com/2013/07/it-begins-pedophiles-call-for-same-rights-as-homosexuals/) *(I would say your desire to have sex with kids is the penalty you are living with....Sick! – Gus Booth)*

For you as a reader of this book you obviously are interested in fighting the battle between sexual freedom and religious freedom, but can I also ask that you be an evangelist for the cause as well. The battle is not just for freedom of speech (though that would be enough to get me to fight) it is also a battle to protect our children and the preaching of the message that "Jesus Saves."

About the Author

Pastor Gus Booth was born in Tracy, MN, raised in Oceanside, CA, graduated from high school in Strongsville, OH, came to a faith in Jesus in Akita, Japan while attending Minnesota State University, and graduated from Bemidji State University, Bemidji, MN.

Pastor Gus Booth first got his feet wet in the ministry through multiple short term mission trips that include over a dozen countries to share the message that "Jesus Saves."

He started pastoring a group of twenty people in Warroad, MN, on January 1, 2001. That group has turned into Warroad Community Church and has over 200 active members in a town of 1,781 souls.

In 2008 national attention came his way when he challenged the IRS' unconstitutional ban on what pastors can say from their pulpit. He was thrust into a battle that is not yet complete. Through multiple interviews with Fox News Channel, NPR, ABC, and almost every major newspaper in the nation he has taken the mantle of free speech to the next level with this book. Enjoy his hard hitting yet loving writing style that mimics his preaching.

He invites you to follow him on Facebook and Twitter @GusBooth

He is married to an awesome wife; they have four children.

To contact the author for speaking engagements call: 218-386-3557.

For further information on Gus Booth please visit www.gusbooth.org

For further information on protecting the gospel please visit www.protectthegospel.com

CPSIA information can be obtained at www.ICGtesting.com
Printed in the USA
LVOW09s2027190215

427263LV00008B/5/P